FAMILY

CAMPING

FAMILY
CAMPING

EVERYTHING YOU
NEED TO KNOW
FOR A NIGHT
OUTDOORS WITH
LOVED ONES

CHARLIE ESS

PHOTOGRAPHS BY CHERYL ESS

FALCON®
GUILFORD, CONNECTICUT

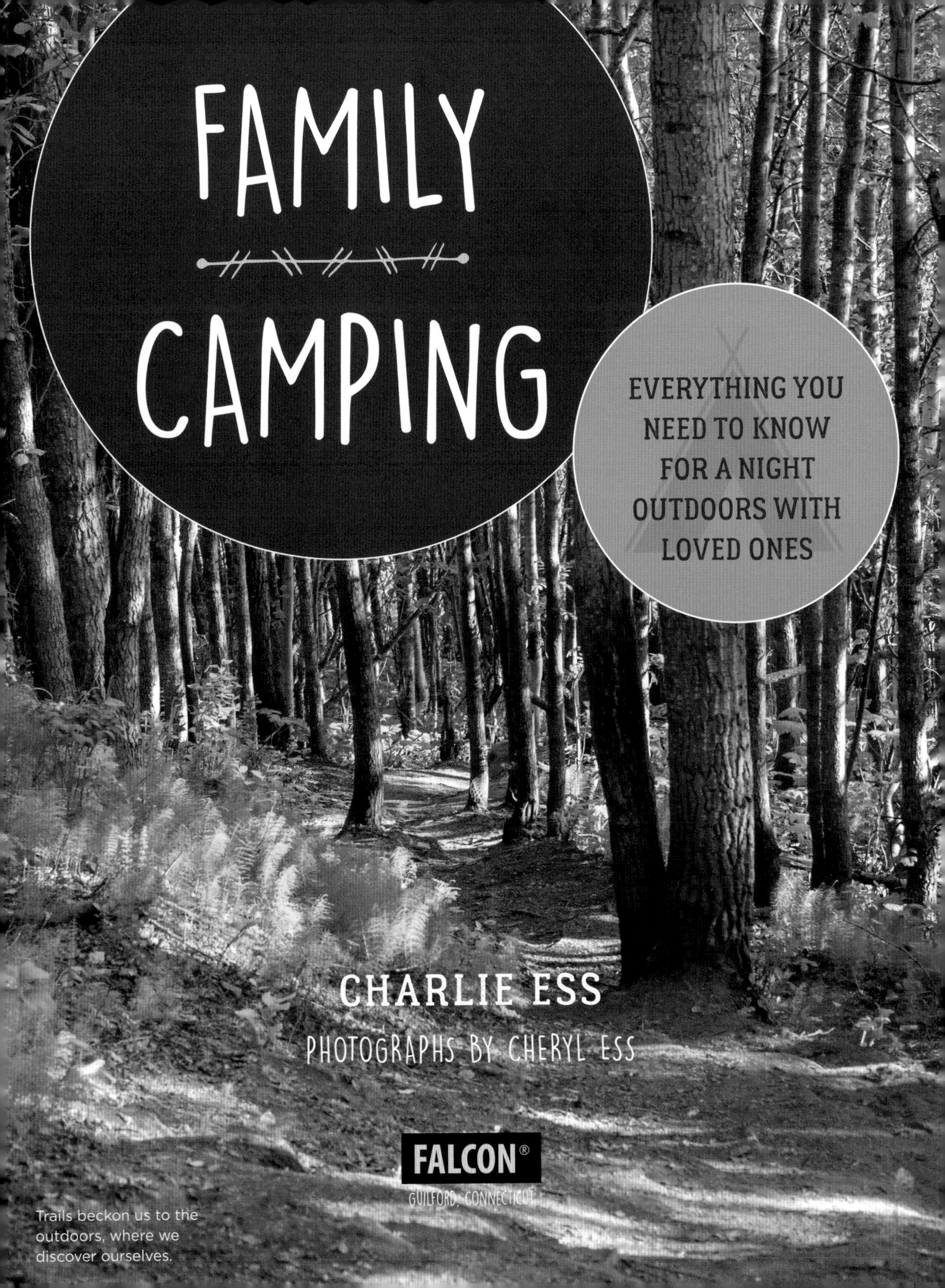

Trails beckon us to the
outdoors, where we
discover ourselves.

FALCON®

An imprint of The Rowman & Littlefield Publishing Group, Inc.
4501 Forbes Blvd., Ste. 200
Lanham, MD 20706
www.rowman.com
Falcon and FalconGuides are registered trademarks and Make Adventure Your Story is a trademark of The Rowman & Littlefield Publishing Group, Inc.

Distributed by NATIONAL BOOK NETWORK

Copyright © 2020 The Rowman & Littlefield Publishing Group, Inc.

Photos by Cheryl Ess

British Library Cataloguing in Publication Information available

Library of Congress Cataloging-in-Publication Data available

ISBN 978-1-4930-4524-2 (paper : alk. paper)
ISBN 978-1-4930-4525-9 (electronic)

∞™ The paper used in this publication meets the minimum requirements of American National Standard for Information Sciences—Permanence of Paper for Printed Library Materials, ANSI/NISO Z39.48-1992.

The identification, selection, and processing of any wild plant for use as food requires reasonable care and attention to details since, as indicated in the text, certain parts are wholly unsuitable for use and, in some instances, are even toxic. Because attempts to use any wild plants for food depend on various factors controllable only by the reader, the author and The Rowman & Littlefield Publishing Group, Inc., assume no liability for personal accident, illness, or death related to these activities.

We dedicate this book to our parents, Kenneth and Annabelle Ess,
and Jerre Wills and Marjorie Torgerson for instilling the
love of woods, lakes, and mountains, and teaching us
how to spend comfortable nights out in the wild.

Camping families are defined by an eclectic
mix of immediate family members and
friends whose love for the outdoors brings
them together for food, fire, and fun.

CONTENTS

The camping experience opens new horizons for young families.

INTRODUCTION

ON A STORMY NIGHT in the dead of winter in Alaska, I find myself smack in the middle of the continuum. I'm curled up inside a huge goose-down bag, which has been tucked inside a nylon bivouac sack that includes a series of three light poles to give it a bit of loft. I am in a party of a dozen cross-country skiers who set out to ski 22 miles, camp out for the night, and return the next day. The wind began blowing in the morning and built to a crescendo by early afternoon. Drifting snow turned all but four of us around just before dark.

I zip the sleeping bag all the way up, which stops a draft blowing down my collar and the hollow of my back. Outside, the wind shrieks through a band of dead cottonwood trees. The temperature has fallen to 4 below. The bright beam of my headlamp reveals that the vestibule of my little tent is already drifted shut with snow.

I settle into my bag, content that I'm exactly where I want to be, that I'm camping for camping's sake and that my predicament here has not been a compromise in the guise of accomplishing something else. Through the years, camping continues its role as the overarching activity in my hunting, fishing, and explorational forays. Though I might fail in my attempts to bag game, catch fish, or conquer the top of a distant mountain, the chores, the fires, the cooking, and the sleeping associated with camping never fail to deliver a huge sense of satisfaction.

We live in a fortunate era when it comes to camping, as the pendulum has swung from "have to" to "want to." Something got lost in the long haul from rolling ourselves up inside animal skins as primitive hunters, and we've made great progress toward the convenience of weathertight houses, the hum of modern appliances, and the infinite array of electronic entertainment. Not that we'd want to go back to sheer survival and our prehistoric ways, but thankfully we're making our way back to the outdoors and have come to recognize camping's merits for the transformational experiences it provides.

While we've titled this book *Family Camping*, this is truly a book for all. Whether you're camping solo (perfect for clearing the mind before making important business or other life-changing decisions) or yearning for an activity that will build relationships with your spouse, children, siblings, or friends, this book is for you. The definition of "family" these days is what you make of it: parents and kids, a gaggle of siblings on a reunion, an outing with members of an extended family—or just a bunch of friends. Read this book straight through or browse its sections for the handy how-tos of camping. Or look for the "Charlie Goes Camping" sidebars scattered throughout for fun anecdotes from my own camping experiences. Whether you're a seasoned camper or trying it for the first time, this guide will take you far down the trail toward the transformational experience of a night out with loved ones in the outdoors, one that will be passed down through the generations. My nephews embarked upon a camping-canoeing trip with their 4- and 5-year-old daughters to instill a love of nature in their most formative years—that and to build lifelong connections of trust with their dads.

If you are brand-new to the activity and not sure of all it demands, it helps to think of camping as a continuum that stretches from cuddling under a blanket with your kiddos on the carpet of your living room all the way to hunkering down together for the night under a pine tree in the Rocky Mountains. The secret, deep down, lies in changing the environment. It's that simple.

 CHARLIE GOES CAMPING

My parents can be credited with my introduction to camping; already in the 1960s they recognized its merits of combining the miracles of nature with a concerted effort to find comfort in the elements—an equation that produces positive family structure.

I'll never forget my first night sleeping out in an olive-drab army surplus tent, how my young legs had never run so much as I explored the woods the day before—and how the cramping in my calves woke me up early the next morning. I lay there, rubbing my legs, and suddenly it hit me: the blended scents of the musty canvas tent, the soil, the sweet aroma of wildflowers and red pine. Though it wasn't yet daylight, the woods were already riotous with the morning calls of songbirds. By the next year, our overnight abode had evolved from a heavily waxed cotton army tent to a rendition from Sears Roebuck, which was lighter-gauge canvas and came in an uplifting sky blue. The 10 × 18-foot tent proved capacious enough to accommodate all seven of us in comfort. In the years to unfold, we acquired lanterns, cots, and camping cookstoves. As we siblings grew up and raised families of our own, the core experience remained the same: Camping still beckons us to come together at a place in the outdoors, to hold ourselves captive to one another, and to experience nature on its own terms.

A couple prepares for
a weekend of solitude
in the woods.

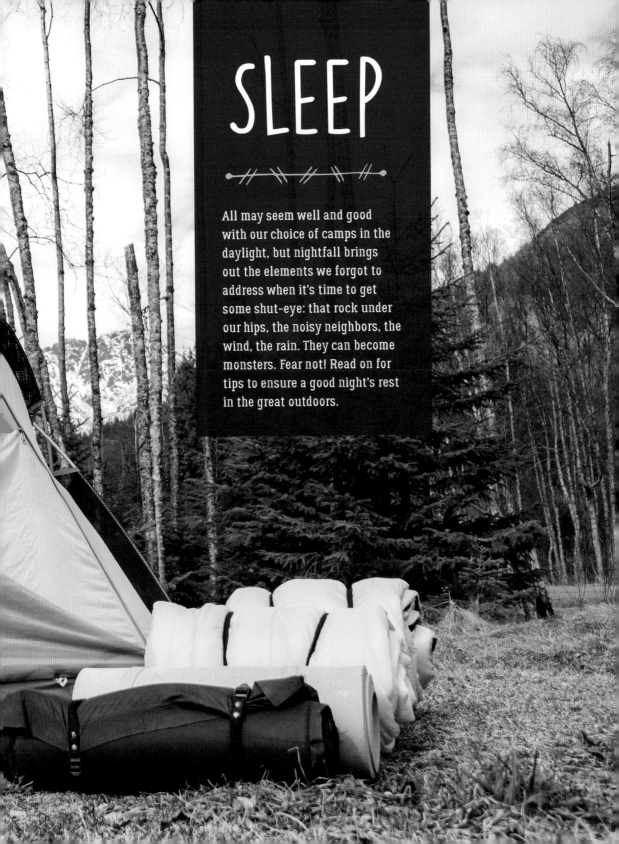

SLEEP

All may seem well and good with our choice of camps in the daylight, but nightfall brings out the elements we forgot to address when it's time to get some shut-eye: that rock under our hips, the noisy neighbors, the wind, the rain. They can become monsters. Fear not! Read on for tips to ensure a good night's rest in the great outdoors.

Chalky gray water and the lack of trees in a wide margin on either side of this creek means it can swell to four times its volume in just minutes after a severe rainstorm.

CHAPTER 1

CHOOSING LOCATIONS

"NOT HERE." That was Kathy's assertion that the guys in the group hadn't considered the element of safety in their choice of the perfect campsite for the night. "If it gets windy, trees could fall on us."

She was one of six students, three young women and three young men, participating in a weeklong hike through the mountains of south-central Alaska. I led the group as part of an outdoor program to promote wilderness skills and leadership. Three days into the trip, the gaggle of students that had been whining about the lack of sunshine and a few mosquitoes back at the trailhead had morphed into a group that had begun to embrace, if not love, the challenge of the elements. They shared in the chores and had already subscribed to the compassion of taping one another's feet to prevent blisters.

"But we need to be closer to water," countered David. He was the daredevil in the group and by far the most outspoken representative of the young men. The rules had been set: The women slept in one tent, the men in another. I set up my own tent in between.

Close distances between camping neighbors can provide positive experiences—or negative—depending on your camping style.

"Plus, we need a more open space to watch for bears." Kathy wasn't letting up.

"But our legs are tired," scowled David, "and we're not hiking all the way down here to pack water back up on that ridge."

It had been a long day. Weariness had set in. They looked at me, their eyes seeking arbitration or any other process that would settle the matter. As an outdoor instructor, I had been well trained in mediating group stalemates: I looked at them, spun on my heels, and walked away.

By then they already knew the drill, and their eyes rolled when I called out over my shoulder that they should send a delegate down the trail to get me when they had agreed upon a campsite. I could only smile with pride as I hiked out of earshot of the group. They were solving problems on their own. Better yet, the combined intelligence of the group would come up with the safest, driest, most convenient place to camp.

LOCATION

As it turns out, camping provides the perfect platform upon which to build leadership within families. A great beginning is to delegate certain tasks among family members, as this instills ownership in the experience. I have met some who leave all the major camping decisions in a given day to one family member and rotate those duties among siblings and parents throughout the week. As the family camping dynamic evolves, try expanding the leadership to taking turns planning the entire trip.

What is it that we demand from a camp? To some families, selecting a place to crash for the night might sound similar to buying a home. Instead of proximity to

 CHARLIE GOES CAMPING

Chores. When you were an adolescent, the term had always meant something you had to do before you got to do the things you wanted. I grew up with four younger siblings whose names fell beneath mine in a vertical column on a sheet of paper tacked to the door of our refrigerator. To the right of our names, Mom had assigned various tasks—washing dishes, rinsing dishes, drying dishes, etc. There were floors to sweep, beds to make, laundry, and dusting. That was our life at home in the suburbs of a Midwestern town, but chores took on a new meaning, a new value, in the early years we went camping. I was the oldest, the biggest, and proud that I had the strength to stuff all seven of the giant rectangular sleeping bags tightly into their large canvas stuff stacks.

My dad had also assigned to me the task of folding the lightweight aluminum cots and stacking them neatly into the gaps between the seats in an aluminum boat, with the sleeping bags nestled tightly together on top. My siblings had the tasks of packing bath towels, toiletries, pillows, food, and other goods in preparation for our weekly trips. It was all part of an intricate process to prepare for camping trips of several days or more in Minnesota's Chippewa National Forest. I was in charge of several other tasks once we arrived at our campsite, and I'd be the one to repack the bags and cots into the trailer for the return trip to town. At the age of 10, I'd discovered purpose through those chores. Little did I know that camping would become the conduit to a work ethic that served me well in the half century that followed. These days, I am reminded of my first chore each time I stuff a sleeping bag.

schools, shopping, and jobs, however, these families scout for the perfect place to pitch the tent for access to fishing, swimming, trailheads for hiking, or local activities such as family reunions, rodeos, state fairs, air shows, or Fourth of July celebrations. Some campgrounds have climbing walls, playgrounds, or natural attractions of their own. But first, pay attention to the elements.

Wind

In the beginning of the search, safety should prevail. Kathy was on the right track with her assessment of the trees in the forested area in which we hiked. The combination of high winds and big tree limbs overhead not only spells imminent danger should one fall on your tent, but the loss of sleep that comes with a breeze and thoughts of the woody biomass hanging overhead just isn't worth it. The other extreme—pitching a tent in an open meadow or on an expansive plain during a windstorm—alleviates concerns of getting crushed by trees or falling debris but leaves the camper exposed. Extremely high winds, around 50 miles per hour, can break even the stoutest of tent poles, leaving the inhabitants to weather the night in a large waterlogged nylon cocoon. I've been there; maybe you have too: lying on your back, holding the waterlogged tent and tarp overhead with your elbow while your camping partner bails water from the floor of the tent with a hiking boot. Over the years, these experiences rate at the bottom of the scale when it comes to my camping aesthetic, and today I take every precaution to avoid high winds and severe rainstorms at the first sight of dark clouds.

The middle ground for such conditions is to pitch a tent for the night in the lee (downwind) side of shrubs or trees that grow in clusters but don't attain much height. Most states have species of willows or alders that serve well as windbreaks, especially in the backcountry. Many established campgrounds have the elements in mind and offer time-tested locations that protect tents from wind.

Assess the campsite for fallen or falling trees. Look for areas clear of trees but protected from wind by distant trees or other vegetation.

Water

Last time I checked, 71 percent of the Earth's surface is composed of water. Depending on our hydration situation, our bodies can be composed of up to 60 percent water. But when it comes to camping, the significance of water jumps to 100 percent. We're talking here about water and your camping location (we'll get to proper hydration later in this book). Water in the wrong place at the wrong time can turn a family camping trip sour, if not deadly; the right amount in the

Onshore winds and high tides
can drive salt water miles inland
during a big storm. Some states
offer camping opportunities
right on the beach. Watch your
weather and check tide tables
before you set up camp.

right place, however, can turn your trip ethereal. As the youth group had already learned on our trip, the proximity of water to the camp demands multiple considerations when it comes to sleeping, recreation, drinking, and hygiene. Let's dive into some extremes.

BEWARE THE GULLY WASHER

I have been to "Dry Creek" here in Alaska and to a "Dry Creek" in Montana; you probably know of one or two in your state. Although these dry creeks live up to their name most days or nights of the year, the night they don't is no night to be sleeping within a mile of their banks. These creeks offer incredible places to camp, however, with their stunning views, expansive sand beaches, and gravel bars heaped with interesting rocks and firewood. Though they can be violent when

 ## CHARLIE GOES CAMPING

My first encounter with Alaska's Dry Creek came after a long day of driving and a failed attempt to meet a friend for what could have turned out to be an entire winter of camping on the Yukon River. Local campgrounds near the area had been closed for more than a month, and the obvious solution to grabbing a little shut-eye involved driving my four-wheel-drive pickup off the highway, dropping it into super low gear, and lurching onto the cobbles of the riverbed. In the high beams of my headlights, I could not find a trickle of water anywhere. As I drove the truck in a figure eight to survey my surroundings, I could only marvel at the power of a creek that could in a few hours gouge the land 0.5 mile wide and leave it strewn with boulders the size of my head.

But there were stars in the sky and it was cold, well below freezing. This Dry Creek would not rage tonight. I pulled out a thin sleeping pad, laid it diagonally across the hood of the truck, grabbed my sleeping bag, and laid on my back. The heat of the engine rose through the thin metal hood, and I relished its warmth in my bag. I might have fallen asleep quickly if not for the appearance of the northern lights. They danced all night, occasionally dipping so close to the Earth that they seemed like fiery green and purple fingers trying to pluck me up and take me to the heavens. I rose the next morning, not well rested but elated with the feeling that I had lived a lifetime in a night. That's what camping does. That's what it's all about.

Heavy rains will test your skills in picking campsites that offer ample drainage.

inundated with runoff, there's a way to play them: Watch for dark clouds on the horizon; if the sky is clear, it's a go, but in areas where weather changes quickly you've got to remain both attentive and mobile.

For starters, don't camp near the middle of the creek bed, and be sure to remember your escape route. Having to drive the family vehicle around a series of gravel bars and weave your way through the landscape for an hour could prove fatal in the event of a flood.

Forgo setting up a tent—you'll want to make fast tracks for higher ground at the first splat of a raindrop. Don't be tricked by drizzle; there may be a torrential downpour at the headwaters miles away. That's how these things work: They can produce millions of cubic feet of water in minutes.

RAIN

In some areas of the country, meteorological data and the stories of the local residents support the theory that there is a rainy season and that the season can be avoided. But the truth in camping is that rain is often an integral part of the outdoor experience—and with the right attitude, it often becomes a great source of fun.

Drainage is the key when setting up the tent or sleeping in a lowland or other depression that promises to fill with standing water when it rains. Try reading the terrain. You want the most level place to rest, but if that spot lies carpeted in ferns or other water-loving vegetation, you might think again. Even if you don't know your plant species, you can decipher what happens when it drizzles. Or when it downpours. Lush mosses and low plants suggest that the area holds water. The appearance of coarse gravel or even rocks among the soft grass indicates an area that funnels moving water when it rains. Areas containing high concentrations

CHARLIE GOES CAMPING

The summer my son, Clarence, was 9, I bought him a small kayak with the idea of portaging through the Nancy Lakes State Recreation Area on two-day forays camping and fishing for the resident northern pike. He was strong for his age, a great fly fisherman already, and though the bright red boat dwarfed him, he made great headway as we paddled and portaged en route to our camping spot. It had been raining hard a few days earlier, but the weather had turned sunny and clear that morning, and the outlook called for more of the same.

I had bought a brand-new heavy-duty space blanket that week in case the ground hadn't dried out completely by the time we camped. As nightfall loomed, we hauled out on a long but level-looking patch of muskeg and found a suitable spot to sleep. Those years I preferred to sleep in a floorless nylon pyramid tent, and for good measure I stretched out the new space blanket under our pads and sleeping bags. The sky remained clear as we crawled in. It was full-on summer. There would be no darkness.

We're accustomed to a few lumps and bumps under our beds when we settle in, and I was amazed that my bed became increasingly softer as the night wore on. I woke to the sound of sloshing water at around 5 a.m. and realized that Clarence and I were sleeping in a 7-acre waterbed. The edges of the thick space blanket had folded upward around us with the rising water. I sat upright, which made the edges of the blanket rise even higher. I slid my hand under Clarence's sleeping bag. Bone dry. I donned my rubber boots, stepped out over the edge, and waded toward the shoreline of the lake. Though the weather had been hot and dry for a day, the latent runoff from the previous rains continued to flow down the gradual slope. We had instant oatmeal, coffee, and cocoa that morning after I devised a pile of stones to keep my backpacking stove above water. We broke camp, launched the kayaks, and caught fish like we'll never forget.

Large surf, dark clouds, and wind portend a night of stormy weather.

of clay may have a soft surface, with millions of cracks suggesting a parched mini desert, but beware of the rains that can turn that "desert" into a sprawling lake overnight. If the area seems devoid of vegetation and sports dry sand, you're in for the simultaneous pleasure of good drainage and a soft bed. Different regions of the country have a mixture of different soils, and most private and public campgrounds have been landscaped with drainage considerations in mind.

But it never hurts to trench. A small plastic shovel or trowel works wonders for digging a small drainage canal around the tent—and the tool may become the primary source of entertainment for young children, who seem to devote hours to creating mud castles and other dirt-derived structures to suit their imaginations.

If you're hoofing it into the wilds, you may encounter muskeg swamps and other low-lying areas that offer the combination of soft and level spots to sleep and low shrubs that provide shelter from the wind. They're readily defined by a flat sleeping area to accommodate a two- or three-person tent and have little depressions all around. These rate among our favorite remote campsites in our home state of Alaska. They have natural drainage during all but the most incessant rainstorms. When it rains for two or three days, however, these areas are subject to water running off the uplands above; we have emerged from our tent to find the trenches filled with a foot of water.

TIDES

To some, beach camping offers the ultimate blend of ocean, beachcombing, fresh breezes, and soft sands sifting between the toes. Choosing locations near coastal areas often adds the extra dimension of having to know the tides. Most local seaside communities have printed copies of tide tables (often a small pamphlet) for the area, but several versions of these tables are available as downloads to your phone. Though tides rise and fall each day, they escalate and fall in series of about a week relative to the pull of the moon. Not to get too technical here, but in the course of a few days in a building series, each high tide usually gets higher than the previous day's high tide until it reaches its apex; then it recedes at roughly the same rate. Determining how high the water will come at the top of the flood and gauging the proper distance from water's edge to the camp on a given night is paramount for safety as well as comfort, but it can also provide a fun and memorable experience for families, especially homeschoolers who like to incorporate their personal experiences in nature into science and math curricula.

When setting up camp in a tidal location, consider both the time and height of the water at high tide and the wind direction. Onshore winds generally raise the water higher on a high tide, while the inverse is true of an offshore wind.

An intrinsic part of calculating a safe distance from the rising water lies in knowing the tides and gauging the wind. Is it onshore or offshore? How strong is

CHARLIE GOES CAMPING

Cheryl and I learned a wet lesson about the idiosyncrasies of tides. We'd been trying to reach an outer saltwater bay with an open boat on one of the Aleutian Islands when huge waves and brisk winds drove us back inside a narrow strait and to the protection of a small cove. The winds increased but the air was dry. As darkness set in, we decided to forgo setting up a tent and elected to sleep on a sandy beach well above the high-tide mark. I toss and turn a fair amount in a night while camping, but I'll never forget the sensation of having drenched feet early that next morning. I sat up and realized that water was sloshing above my knees. I had grossly misjudged the high tide. It took days to dry out my bag and wet clothing.

Rivers with expansive gravel bars indicate that they flood to capacity during sudden heavy rains.

it blowing? How deep is the ocean offshore? If you're on the East Coast and the wind blows from the east, it may raise the water even higher than the maximum height the tide tables predict. Seaside camping and the tides hold rich adventure for families. Walking the beach at low tide often yields treasures in the form of sea creatures caught in tide pools, and each tide often leaves interesting flotsam that can include glass bottles from afar, beautiful seashells, starfish, and the shells of crabs and other creatures.

Sun

Sunshine is great when you need it to dry out tents and wet clothing or to warm up the morning chill, but too much sun can ruin your trip and compromise your health. Depending on the latitude and the season in which you're camping, the sun swings through a predictable arc through the sky in the course of the day. Here in Alaska, the summer sun swings in a giant arc, never really rising and never really setting. Its intensity warrants sunscreen, particularly if we're out on the water, but we've noticed that if we travel to the Midwest or West, we start turning red with just a couple hours of sun on our shoulders. Generally, the sun reaches its maximum intensity between the hours of 10 a.m. and 2 p.m.

Your complexion has much to do with how you handle exposure to the sun. Some folks may have conditioned themselves with time out on daily runs, cleaning the swimming pool, or mowing the lawn, but the prolonged exposure that often comes with camping trips can hold unpleasant surprises if they're not prepared. Options for protection range from seeking the shade of trees or other foliage near campsites to applying varying strengths of sunscreen to wearing hats with long visors to protect the nose and face. Another option is to tuck the tail of a large handkerchief under the back of a hat so that the material extends to cover the neck.

Neighbors

For a good part of our lives—pre-children—we camped for entire summers alone; our neighbors were the whales, sea lions, bears, wolves, and eagles. We would not learn the importance of choosing locations with an emphasis on our *Homo sapiens* neighbors until years later, when we set up our tent in public or private campgrounds with young children of our own. We entered the family camping scene and learned of incidents in which firewood had been stolen, coolers had been raided, or axes or other tools had been pilfered by other campers. Heck, we were young once too, and we contributed our fair share to transforming the word "party" from a noun to a verb; we also did due diligence in making that word synonymous with "camping."

But that wasn't the experience we were looking for, not as parents to young children.

If that's not yours either, consider integrating these handy tips into selecting your next campsite.

DISTANCE BETWEEN CAMPSITES AND FROM AMENITIES

Public and private campgrounds reap more revenue by packing more campsites into a given acre. In terms of aesthetics, however, that can equate to overcrowding. A sure sign that things are a bit tight is when neighbors ask to tie one of their tent guylines onto one of your tent stakes—or when you hear the intimacies of a marital dispute through the thin walls of your tent. On the other hand, tight spacing between tents works great when you're leading groups or chaperoning the youth of multiple families—or when you prefer to camp around others for security against strangers or weather calamities.

As you discover new places to camp, you'll become familiar with a variety of regulations relating to such things as the discharge of firearms, liquor consumption, "quiet hours," and other rules of conduct—or the lack thereof. Some states may have "sacrificial" lands—abandoned gravel pits or highway pullouts that see little upkeep or improvements. These areas are often unregulated. On the plus

 CHARLIE GOES CAMPING

When I was a child in Minnesota, my family reached a consensus of our favorite campsite—in one of four campgrounds surrounding Lake Winnibigoshish in the Chippewa National Forest. The criteria included proximity to our fishing boat, which was pulled up onshore near our camp each night; access to good sand on the bottom of the lake for wading and swimming; the 100-yard distance to the outdoor bathrooms; seclusion from our neighbors; and a distance of about 150 yards to a hand-pumped well, which supplied our potable water. Summers were busy times around the lakes in northern Minnesota, and our perfect campsite wasn't always available. We'd settle for vacant sites, but always at a compromise: Too close to the bathrooms meant a lot of foot traffic and noise near our camp. That also meant packing our water an extra 200 yards, and we couldn't see our boat from the tent.

This same campground offered paths between campsites. They averaged about 25 yards long and stayed well-worn from foot traffic. As we settled into the rhythm of our summers, we noticed ourselves among families of similar structure in terms of ages and interests. In time we began chumming with other kids when we were swimming in the lake, and soon the paths came into their own as we made friends in neighboring camps. In many ways, the physical layout of that campground taught us to socialize.

side, because there are no services, there are no camping fees.

Campsites in some parks and national monuments may require making reservations or getting permits months ahead. Folks wanting a campsite from June to September in Yellowstone National Park, for example, are advised to make reservations six months to a year in advance.

DISTANCE FROM VEHICLE

Another worthwhile consideration is the distance from the campsite to your vehicle. To provide more room in the tents, cameras, electronic devices, hunting or fishing gear, and other valuables are often best left locked in the trunk or otherwise out of sight in vehicles overnight, but that sometimes leaves those same valuables vulnerable to theft. Some campgrounds offer parking for cars at individual campsites; others require parking in a central lot. What stays in the tent and what stays in your vehicle will evolve according to your needs.

Bears are a treasure; storing food properly keeps them in that status— and not a nuisance.

In nearly all campgrounds, coolers containing food and beverages should stay overnight in your vehicle. Most states have raccoons, skunks, and even bears that have wisened up to the goodies stored within coolers. Some campgrounds have incorporated locking steel boxes to store food and other supplies away from animals. Raccoons are among the smartest, most dexterous animals; I've always marveled at their skill in figuring out how to unlatch various containers. It pays to ensure that your food and other tantalizingly aromatic supplies have been locked in the trunk of your vehicle.

Accessible Sites

Most American campgrounds offer wheelchair access to tent pads, as well as access to bathrooms, showers, and other amenities. But it never hurts to check ahead of time to ensure that camping arrangements have you close to bathrooms and shower facilities, potable water, better views, and easy access to beaches, wheelchair-accessible trails, and sightseeing opportunities. That might mean making reservations to secure particular campsites that offer these amenities.

Campsites for people with disabilities should put campers within easy proximity of water supplies, bathrooms, and other amenities. This one borders a paved hiking trail along the coast in Seward, Alaska.

Darkness

Unless you're camping in the arctic regions of Alaska between late April and mid-August, you will encounter darkness. After decades of living and camping in the far north, I was amazed at how fast the sun went down when we went camping in Montana. Turns out, the time between sunset and total darkness decreases proportionate to your latitude. Hawaii, for instance, sits at about 24 degrees north, and that big sun sinks over the horizon at an alarming rate compared to 67 degrees north in Alaska, where it descends in a long slicing arc across the horizon for hours, sets for about an hour, and then rises again.

In the mid latitudes—40 to 50 degrees north—a trick we used as kids was to extend an arm straight out in front, tuck in the thumb, rotate the hand to a

A full moon in any
season means less
darkness at night.

vertical position, curl the fingers 90 degrees so that they form a stack, then place the bottom of the little finger on the horizon. Each finger represented 15 minutes before sunset. If the sun was above the index finger, we had more than an hour; if it was below the index finger, we peeled our fingers back to estimate how much time we had before darkness enveloped the land. Nowadays, there are many phone apps that will tell you the precise time of sunrise and sunset.

Even with an accurate measure of remaining daylight, however, we've frequently been caught out in the dark, which means we have a wide array of headlamps, flashlights, LED (light-emitting diode)lanterns and batteries, a candle lantern—even several old white-gas lanterns with mantles.

When it's time to choose your camp lighting, think of multiple sources, not just one. Headlamps are a must for having hands free for trekking poles or for that late-night sojourn down to the creek to fetch water. Most headlamps use

LEDs and have a bulb life of more than 70,000 hours. I have a couple headlamps with bulbs that promise to function for more than a decade; I can only hope to live long enough to see the bulb burn out on one I recently purchased.

Batteries, on the other hand, can die within hours, and the more lumens (brightness) an LED lamp puts out, the shorter the battery life.

The biggest culprit that can leave you groping about in the dark is having the switch of a headlamp, flashlight, or other source of lighting inadvertently get bumped to the "on" position in your duffel or backpack. When shopping for headlamps, look for models in which the switch can be made inaccessible by tilting the lamp down tight toward the headband or can be disarmed by holding the switch down for 5 seconds. Many manufacturers offer rechargeable headlamps, but even they'll do you no good if they've been blazing away in the bottom of your backpack hours before dark. Place headlamps or flashlights in your outer pockets so that other items within the pack don't accidentally turn on the switch.

If protected or time-delayed switches are not available, a great hack is to switch one of the batteries end-for-end within the lighting pack. This prevents a complete circuit and prevents the bulb from lighting up. A slight downside to this method is that you'll have to remember how to arrange the batteries so that you can turn your light on when it gets dark.

Look for other features when you purchase a headlamp, such as models that offer choices in high or low power settings and wide or narrow beams.

While some campers prefer to stay ultralight and hang their headlamps from twigs or overhead tent loops to create the effect of a lantern, new generations of mini lanterns have handy hangers and bulb designs that disperse light over a broader area than the narrow beams of headlamps. Like many headlamps, these lanterns also allow you to set the intensity of the light.

For those nostalgics out there, some backpacking and outdoor supply stores still sell collapsible candle lanterns. These come with a protective globe of glass. You insert a long-burning candle (they last about 10 hours), sold at the same stores, light it up, and hang it a safe distance from the inside roof of the tent. As you might expect, these lanterns put out 1 candlepower, so things might seem a bit dim, especially if you're trying to find a lost contact lens or other small object. They also put out a bit of heat and drive minute traces of moisture out of the tent.

Lightweight backpacking/
bicycling tents provide
suitable shelter in the
mountains.

CHAPTER 2

SHELTER, CLOTHING, AND PERSONAL GEAR

YOU'VE FOUND YOUR CAMPSITE and shut off the car. The dog has been whining for the last 20 miles, and the kids have complained since the last time you stopped for gas. They need to get out and run. Hit the unlock button, and open the doors to your new adventure. Step out, stretch, and take a moment to let it sink in. This is your environment for the next day or two or, if you're lucky, maybe a week. As kids, the agreement when we arrived at this juncture of the trip was that we could run down to the lake, spend a few minutes, then run back to our campsite and embrace the next crucial stage of camping: setting up shelter. If the lake beckoned and we stayed a bit long, we'd hear our cue to return: the metallic ringing of my dad's hammer on long steel pegs as he drove in the corner stakes of our massive tent.

SHELTER BASICS

Let's back up a bit, to months or even a year before, when you defined what it is you'll need as a suitable tent and all the accoutrements contained within. Shopping for a tent as a family might well provide great fun and an alternative to board games in the doldrums of winter. When it comes to choices in basic structures, the number of bodies sprawled within its confines at bedtime will ultimately determine the size of the tent's footprint.

Mom, Dad, and the five of us siblings got by comfortably in a 10 × 18-foot canvas tent. The decision to buy that particular canvas cabin tent had been solidified the year before when my dad borrowed the same model from a friend for our very first family outing—you might find similar opportunities to try before you buy. Sleeping is but one facet of the total camping experience. The peripheral activities of cooking, bathing, and hobbies enter the equation and may predicate the addition of a large tarp or screen tent to your package. As our camping experience evolved, we added a 12 × 12-foot screen tent for cooking and for a place to hang out when it rained. The screen tent had no floor, which meant we could easily pitch it to enclose a large wooden campground picnic table. Its top was heavy waterproof canvas, which kept out rain, and the majority of its sidewalls were fine-meshed bug screen. We spent more time in the screen tent than in the sleeping tent, and such additional living space may be a consideration in your planning.

As the decades have slipped by, we've owned no fewer than nine tents. That might seem like a lot, but, hey, we love camping. A significant influence in what we buy comes from our observations in campgrounds during high-volume events such as the Fourth of July. Though we've flocked like countless others to the seaside town of Seward for a few days of camping, it's like a living trade show, a parade of tents. For years we've observed trends in the newest fabrics, innovative pole systems, and the progression of different geometric shapes. The industry has gone to great lengths to offer solid product lines, replete with eye-grabbing colors. But we've also seen some traditional canvas models and even tepees with long wooden poles.

TENTS

Today's tents come in all shapes and sizes. Floor plans run the gamut from square to oval to round, elongated hexagons, octagons, and everything in between. Tents with straight vertical walls have been designed to allow campers to stand within; domes that squat waist-high off the ground have been designed with aerodynamics in mind for wind. Such tents limit their inhabitants to maneuvering around on their knees, but we've also seen dome tents with centers high enough to allow standing.

As you incorporate the family dynamic into your tent decision, a worthy discussion is group size and the consideration of friends. As children enter the formative years of middle school and they're no longer satisfied to hang out with parents, the inclusion of friends can be a powerful catalyst to getting great trips off the ground.

Of course this may mean buying more tents. But they'll be smaller—and cheaper—as the boys and girls separate into their respective sleeping units and convene in a larger cook tent or under a large tarp as a main meeting space. Yet another camping-sleeping arrangement discussion might include joining forces with local church groups or outdoor groups that already own the equipment and sponsor large group events, often throughout the summer.

Assuming that you want to maintain the immediate family structure, some primary features to focus on, besides the size tent you'll need, include zippers, poles, fabric, and convenience.

Zippers

While most folks think of zippers in terms of opening and closing jackets, coats, purses, or luggage, nothing quite approximates the length of a zipper traversing the front of a tent. The larger the tent, the larger the zipper, and most tents have the doors configured in a large half-moon radius. That means the slider (the zipper part that gathers the teeth and locks them together when closing the door and reverses the process when you open the door) must scream along two rows of teeth—hundreds of them.

Zipper construction and choices in materials vary widely among manufacturers and also through price ranges for tents. We've seen single- and double-row zippers made of plastic and steel. We've owned tents with zippers composed of tiny teeth and those with large teeth.

When you're shopping, the best test is to pull zippers through on the showroom floor. They should move smoothly and easily—the family camping experience could mean opening and closing them up to one hundred times a day.

Zippers are crucial components of tents and sleeping bags. Inspect them carefully when you buy, and keep sand out of them when you camp.

Through the years, we've discovered that zippers, no matter how smoothly they pull and no matter what they're made of, have a much shorter life if you're camping around sand. The problem with sand falling into zippers is that the grains of sand are roughly twice as hard as the metal components of the zippers. (Think of the difference between steel and a grinding stone.) Wet sand wears down zippers even quicker, as it packs between the teeth and compromises their

CHARLIE GOES CAMPING

We had been dropped off in a remote bay in southwest Alaska with plans on setting up a permanent 8 × 10-foot white-walled canvas tent, which had an internal frame constructed of 2 × 4-inch lumber and fastened together with large bolts and plywood gussets for bracing. It was late in the evening, and with the last of the supplies offloaded and ferried to shore from a large fishing boat, we decided to set up a small 5 × 7-foot backpack tent for the night and resume packing supplies up the hill to our camping spot in the morning. The backpack tent had been lauded as sturdy and waterproof when I'd bought it the summer before, and I'd spent numerous nights out in it, but always within the relative protection of trees. Out here on the naked tundra, I began to have my doubts. We assembled the poles and erected the tent, but the wind was increasing with each passing moment.

With darkness looming, we crawled in. Not a half hour later, a horrendous gust hit us and tore out the two stakes on the windward corners, allowing wind to get under the floor of the tent. The next gust lifted our heads off the ground. The soil was soft and black below us, and nothing I could think of could be driven deep enough to secure the windward edges of the tent. I elected to collect a half dozen football-size rocks from the beach, drag them into the tent with us, and place them in the corners. They held the tent down for the better part of 2 hours. But the wind increased even more, with some gusts hitting 70 miles per hour.

In Alaska we have williwaws, a condition caused by high winds tumbling over the mountains and wreaking havoc in the valleys below. We were in the lee (downwind) side of a

ability to interlock. Shaking the fabric near the zippers can dislodge a lot of the sand, and fastidiously brushing the teeth with an old toothbrush also has merit.

There's another trick to prolonging zipper life, no matter which tent you buy. Traffic in and out of the tent deposits sand within the teeth and does zippers in. To reduce the amount of sand reaching the teeth, lay remnants of carpet or Astroturf near the tent's entrance.

Poles

Like zippers, the next important feature to the tent equation comes in many forms and different materials. Poles are to the rigidity and survival of the tent as the skeleton is to the structure of the human body. Tent manufacturers have

(WITH THE WRONG TENT)

mountain range, and not only does the velocity of a williwaw increase as wind races over the peaks and drops to the valleys below, but it causes turbulence, which translates to seconds of eerie calm followed by an explosive downward gust. We'd been through williwaws before, but never in this particular tent.

Somewhere in the delineation of night and morning a gust hit us so hard that the rainfly popped with the loudness of a gunshot. It left my ears ringing. At least two poles had snapped. Seconds later, another gust rocketed down the mountain, breaking the other two poles and leaving the entire wet mass of nylon to encase us like a giant cocoon. Without the poles to spread the corners of the tent, the wind worked its way under the floor and rolled the rocks against our heads. For hours we lay on our backs with our arms over our faces to keep some airspace between us and the wet nylon. As with most storms, daylight brought respite. Morning eventually dawned with the revelation that we'd survived the night. We crawled out of our wet sleeping bags, resolved to continue our mission of setting up the larger camp. The wind continued at a steady gale throughout the remainder of the day. We donned our rain gear and stayed busy packing supplies up the hill.

In the days that followed, we erected the wall tent and lived in it for another six weeks, through many storms, including one with winds that clocked in at more than 130 miles per hour. The wall tent held up well. We left that remote bay in late August—I promptly tossed the backpack tent into a trash can upon our return to civilization.

always walked a thin line between geometric designs that provide maximum strength against the elements and the ease with which tents can be set up. Through the decades we've seen a pattern in designs toward convenience, especially on models tailored to first-time campers. What that means in terms of pole configuration is that you basically erect a large spider-shaped frame high over the tent, which is laid with its corners stretched taut over the ground. The poles should be snug when fitting them together, and there shouldn't be any wiggle or sloppiness in the joints. Other hardware that joins the poles should fit equally well. Many tents require bending the poles in a slight arc before they'll fit the joining hardware. The next steps require snapping plastic clips over the poles intermittently along the tent's main corner seams. (I'll refrain from jokes about a

Poles are the backbone of your tent. With proper care, they can keep your temporary home comfortable for years.

particular gender and its aversion to reading instructions.) Many of these tent frame setups can be understood intuitively right out of the box. Trust me. And given the multifaceted intelligence of a family, you'll have the tent up in no time.

Tents whose manufacturers boast of their durability in extreme weather, on the other hand, require a bit of thinking in the setup process. These are typically domes or oval-shaped domes, and that pile of skinny poles lying before you will crisscross to form a well-rounded geodesic shape. Generally these tents have far less area between the poles, and the poles slide through fabric sleeves that follow the seams in the tent. These poles may be thinner in diameter than those for the tents described above, but they have been engineered for maximum strength. The ferrules should be tight but smooth as they slide together, and the shock cord that runs through their interior should be tight enough that it doesn't cause loops that hinder assembly. Some manufacturers color-code poles of different lengths to aid in putting them through the proper sleeves in the tent fabric.

By a predictable margin, these geodesic tents will remain standing when entry-level models have been flattened to the ground, but expect to pay a hefty price to cover the cost of the carbon fiber or aluminum alloys going into the pole system. We have owned several of these tents, and have survived nights out in remote stretches of Alaska when the wind blew 100 miles per hour or more.

Fabric

Tent fabric has evolved from the heavily waxed canvas of the 1940s to nylon in the 1970s and continued on a trajectory toward superlight, ultra-tough silicone-based thin veils in 2020. Advances toward the development of lighter, weather-proof materials will likely continue their trend, which favors the shopper in terms of minimizing weight and maximizing protection from rain, mildew, insects, and other elements of camping, but only where quality prevails. Look for internal reinforcement strands in the fabric in the fields between the poles. While the fabric might endure driving rain, snow, wind, and the other elements, construction of the seams and placement of grommets, clips, or other integral pieces could compromise the tent overall. Check the quality of the thread and the stitching. Some manufactures use double and even triple stitching along the seams.

Convenience

Pop-up tents have become a mainstay for car campers who prefer a tent and a campsite to a hotel in long-distance drives across the country. But pop-ups have also won favor among folks who don't want the hassle of assembling elaborate pole systems as part of pitching their tents. These tents, like the name implies, pop up to their full dimensions within seconds after being removed from their stuff sacks. As for shapes, there are pyramids, tepees, domes, elongated domes, and cabin-style tents on the market. Most of these tents are constructed with a single poly skin and have been designed to function without rain tarps. Manufacturers claim that the tent's single layer is sufficiently waterproof, and many customer reviews agree.

Pop-up tents erect within moments; some explode into shape within seconds after being removed from their stuff sacks.

CHARLIE GOES CAMPING

I'll never forget my first overnight in a structure called a wickiup, a tepee-like arrangement with tall poles that had been covered with pine boughs, branches, and dead leaves. It was late January, and I was co-teaching a wilderness survival class for college credits in northern Minnesota.

The previous two nights had been clear and cold, and we'd slept under the stars. But the coming night promised rain, even snow. My lead instructor confided that he knew the location of the shelter, which had been previously erected by another class of students, and that with a little refinement our group of eight could expect to wake up reasonably dry the next morning. Though the other campers had done the work in the primary construction of the shelter, there was much to be done along the lines of plugging gaps and holes in the foliage between the poles. We set about collecting moss and branches of pine and spruce and then settled in for the night. Unlike previous camping experiences, when precipitation pitter-pattered loudly upon the tarp of a tent, the crude shelter remained silent during heavy snow, sleet, and rain that night. The gaps in the shelter also permitted the ambient smells of the forest to creep in, and I remember falling asleep in a newfound intimacy with the elements.

MINIMALIST STYLE

Maybe you don't want a tent at all. Depending on your sense of adventure and the protocols of the private or public lands where you wish to camp, crashing out for a night under the stars or beneath the boughs of coniferous trees might be the experience you've been waiting for. But first check local, regional, and local laws about cutting trees or other vegetation, as it's illegal in national and many state parks. Cutting limbs, branches, and twigs and collecting leaves to build a natural survival shelter brings the rewards of accomplishment, as doing it right often demands elite woodcraft skills. The more you know about knots, local vegetation, weather patterns, and other key ingredients of your surroundings will have a direct correlation between a night of misery or camping out in relative comfort. It's intense—and it's rewarding. A nice way to ease into this camping style is to allow yourself the luxury of a tarp or bivy sack. Even then, this camping style is often unpredictable. It will test old skills and lead to the discovery of new ones.

BAGS

Given the plethora of products on the market, you could spend the rest of your life deciding which sleeping bag to buy. In the beginning of our camping days, bags were simple rectangles consisting of canvas and cotton. They were bulky,

Tents and pads provide extra warmth, but the real test comes from crawling into the sleeping bag after the sun goes down and the fire burns low.

difficult to stuff, and became unmanageable monsters when they got wet. Times have changed with the availability of alternative materials, but those large rectangular bags still have merit in terms of extra room to toss and turn for those of us who fight claustrophobia in the tighter-fitting mummy bags. Most rectangular bags have been constructed symmetrically from right to left, and from top to underside, which allows them to be flipped so that their zippers run on either side. This offers a huge advantage over mummy bags, which are tapered from head to toe and have a distinct top and underside. The beauty is that you can flip rectangular bags so that their zippers are facing each other; moreover, the zippers can be interlocked to form a double-bag setup. We used a combination of two zip-together bags, which gave us enough room to sleep together with our infant babies between us.

Like tents, sleeping bags come in all shapes and sizes.

Already in the 1980s, some manufacturers provided mummy bags with right- or left-hand zippers; we eventually bought two that would zip together for our cold-weather winter camping. The same company also offered their winter bags in varying lengths, and although I stand only 5 foot, 10 inches tall, I purchased an 84-inch model, rated to 40 below zero, with the intention of stuffing one of my sled dogs in with me for extra heat should the arctic night threaten to hit 60 or 70 below.

As a family you may discover individual preferences in shapes, materials, and other features as you peruse the choices at the camping gear store. Though several online outfitters can ship sleeping bags to your door within days, even hours, I'd recommend a hands-on shopping trip to check out bags for their construction materials (synthetics, cotton, down); sizes and shapes; and the quality of zippers, drawstrings, stitching, and other integral features.

CHARLIE GOES CAMPING

"Voyage to the Bottom of the Sleeping Bag." That's what we kids called it as a joke each night before Dad shut off the lantern and we zipped into our oversize rectangular bags. The idea stemmed from the popular TV series *Voyage to the Bottom of the Sea*, which ran for 110 episodes and piped into our black-and-white Zenith through its coat-hanger antenna back in the 1960s. The show featured the travails of a submarine and its crew, who cruised to the uncharted depths of the ocean under the guise of research. Well, we wouldn't be doing any research in our camp at night, but invariably one of us siblings would get turned around, most probably disoriented from deep dreams and sleeping in the fetal position. We'd stretch out and plow our way to the bottom of our bag, thinking we were headed for the top. The resultant panic, shortage of air, and accompanying cries for help would wake our parents, and we'd hear the screaming of a zipper as they intervened and spun us around. If memory serves me correctly, just about every night one of us kids starred in "Voyage to the Bottom of the Sleeping Bag," and it always made for great laughs the next morning.

PADS

There are almost infinite choices in pads, from thin inflatables to huge inflatables, some requiring small air compressors that run off your automobile's battery. There are pads made of closed-cell foam, meaning they won't absorb water; foam pads that rely on the integrity of their outer shells to prevent soaking up water; and pads without waterproof shells that soak up water like a sponge if they are exposed. Thickness also varies widely, and a little research and testing go a long way toward increased comfort when it comes time to camp. Unlike tents and even sleeping bags, pads are highly individualized in terms of thickness and rigidity—or lack thereof—in conforming to your body.

For starters, it helps to identify your sleeping habits at home. If you prefer to sleep on your side and have the latest and greatest adjustable mattress for its hip-saving attributes, you'll probably want a thick inflatable pad for a restful sleep experience at camp.

Pad varieties include inflatables, hard foam, soft foam, and lots of options in between.

If you can sleep in any position, and have been known to crash out comfortably on no more than a carpeted floor, a simple 0.5-inch closed-cell pad might suit you well.

There are also composite pads that encase 2 or more inches of foam inside an inflatable shell. They incorporate a valve or, in some cases, multiple valves and separate air chambers that you can open and inflate with your breath to your preferred firmness. When it feels just right, you close the valve to seal in the air.

Complicating the choices even further is the anticipation of the ground upon which you plan to sleep and the compatibility between the materials on the outside of your pad and the outside of your sleeping bag. I have numerous pads that fit the bill perfectly in terms of comfort, but their outer shell material makes my sleeping bag slip off their edges. When I camp on rough ground, or in winter when my body sinks into the snow beneath the bag, I often find myself sleeping essentially on barren ground with my pad protruding at a weird angle to the side of me. The answer has been to use an underlying tarp and to build a nonskid layer between my bag and pad with my parka, snow pants, and preferably something made of fleece, which grips the bag and keeps me centered on the pad. I discovered all of this out in the woods in the middle of the night, but with a little testing, you can avoid a lot of the surprises in finding the perfect pad.

Though the primary duty of the sleeping pad is to provide comfort at night in the woods, I've met several families who incorporate inflatable air mattresses as part of their recreation on the water. Used properly and in conjunction with a personal flotation device (PFD), or lifejacket, to use old-school vernacular, these pads make great floating toys. They're buoyant; they're fun; and though I could find only references to someone surfing huge waves on an inflatable mattress, I expect to hear of oceanic crossings or trans-world navigation upon one of the pads in the years to come. Air mattresses vary widely in price, and their distinguishing features include the outside material, the number of baffles or chambers, and the size.

Depending on the terrain and other characteristics of the ground at your campsites—and the floor construction of your particular tent—a liner or ground cloth between the pad and the tent increases warmth and protects pads from punctures caused by pebbles or other sharp objects in the ground. These cloths vary from ultrathin Mylar space blankets to plastic-coated tarps to artificial turf or scraps of old carpet. These inexpensive (usually under $20) blankets can prolong the life of pads and make for an even more comfortable night in camp.

COTS

The ultimate lining between you, your sleeping bag, your pad, and the ground would be a cot. Camping cots range from renditions of jointed lawn and patio furniture to ultralight contraptions that require some assembly each time but weigh less than 3 pounds. Among the benefits of elevating your body off the ground, expect added warmth, a rigid and level platform for sleeping, and storage for your gear underneath. The height at which the cot stands off the ground becomes an important consideration if you plan to sleep in a dome tent or in a tent where the angle of the walls tapers inward sharply from the floor to the peak. Given a cot's rigidity and defined edges, it will need to be placed several inches to a foot inside of the tent's fabric walls to avoid contact with and chafing of the fabric when the wind blows. Depending on the dimensions of the cot and the angle of the tent walls, the addition of cots can turn a four-person tent into a two-person tent.

Generally, when shopping for cots, cheaper prices mean cheaper materials and more weight. Look for cots made of steel and stout fabric and weighing more than 10 pounds for prices under $50, and upward of $300 for cots with frames made of titanium, carbon fiber, or other materials with weights of less than 3 pounds.

Hammocks offer a great way to relax with our loved ones at camp.

HAMMOCKS

For the ultimate sleeping setup, hammocks might be the end-all for folks who love to sleep on their backs and a must-have for those of us who don't. Modern camping hammocks compress to the size of a softball and can accommodate sleepers of up to 300 pounds. They'll hold you secure, like a partial cocoon; and if you rig them right in trees on nights when there is a breeze, they'll carry you back, unlocking memories of your mother rocking you to sleep. The trick is to know your knots so that you can rig your hammock tightly between two trees, and it helps to incorporate a separate overhead line between the same two trees. The overhead line supports bug netting and a tarp and makes for a surprisingly comfortable camp—at a fraction of the weight of most other camping gear.

CLOTHING

It may seem a bit odd to group a discussion about clothing into a chapter on where to sleep and what to sleep on, but the right clothing can help you sleep better, regardless of your sleeping gear. First off: layers. You've probably heard it all before, but pay attention to clothing selection, starting from your underwear and working outward toward the elements. With a little thought and planning, the cost of acquiring a good set of layered clothing can be far from prohibitive.

Base Layers

When it comes to the base layer, your underwear, outdoor clothing companies offer a wide array of synthetic blends that wick away sweat when the heat is on so that you stay dry as you cool down. Often these blends are a combination of polyester with another material (spandex) to provide elasticity when you're moving. Merino wool is a favorite undergarment of US Navy SEALS and other military branches wanting to maximize the wick-away qualities, fire-retardant capabilities, and durability of wool. Merino-based clothing will cost more, but many swear by its softness against the body and attest that it doesn't hold body odor like some undergarments made of synthetic blends. In some instances, tops and bottoms are sold as matching sets. Even better, some sets offer short-sleeve or long-sleeve tops.

Middle and Outer Layers

The middle layer of clothing serves as the outer layer in early or late summer in some states or as the outer layer year-round in southern states where ambient daytime and nighttime temperatures don't dip below 60°F. It becomes the middle layer—in our definition—when you're camping in higher latitudes (north) and deserts, where temps can dip below freezing day or night. Mid-layer tops and bottoms offer long sleeves and full-length bottoms and should fit comfortably over your base layer. As you try on your second layer, swing your arms through their entire range of motion to mimic reaching for lines, chopping wood, and other camp chores to ascertain that the two layers don't bunch up uncomfortably at the elbows. For your bottoms, flex your knees and do a couple of squats to determine that your mid-layer doesn't drag the base layer down low on your butt to expose a portion of the body that has been disrespectfully associated with plumbers. Camp chores and associated activities demand maximum flexibility, and clothing that compromises movement just won't do.

Outer layers come in a variety of materials, including synthetic fleeces and fleece jackets or pants contained within wind-stopping or water-resistant shells. More expensive versions of these outer shells incorporate zippers that allow removal of the outer shell from the inner fleece. These are your best friends when the weather turns unexpectedly cool or with the sudden arrival of rain or snow squalls. These should fit comfortably over your middle and under layers to provide flexibility and movement of the arms and legs when hiking or moving about camp.

A heavy cotton hooded sweatshirt makes for an additional outer shell—a perennial favorite around camps and campfires. Acquiring hoodies can be an easy task when you visit local attractions or gift shops along the route to your camping destinations. Many vendors offer a wide selection of sizes and colors as part of their business branding campaigns. Seasoned campers and other travelers often sport a collection of hoodies from the states and iconic places they've visited.

If your camping style does not include backpacking, where cutting down on weight and bulk are paramount, throw in a pair of old jeans or durable work pants for some of the grungier chores around camp. Digging in dirt or mud or removing ashes from campfire rings, outdoor cookers, and grills often leaves large black smudges, and having a "sacrificial" set of clothing will save your other layers for what they do best: keeping you warm and dry.

Hats

Hats come with big brims, small brims, and in myriad styles and colors. Baseball caps are a favorite around intense sun and help cut the glare of the sun off water. Most have adjustable bands in back to fit a wide range of head sizes. Other versions have interior fleece earflaps that can be tucked up inside the hat when

Caps provide warmth around the ears, while hats with bills provide some warmth and protection from the overhead sun.

the weather is warm and dropped down for protection against wind and cold. Though baseball cap bills protect cheeks, nose, and lips from the overhead sun, folks with short hair may notice their necks getting sunburned as the afternoon wears on.

The trick? Throw a handkerchief over the top of your head and adjust it so that most of the cloth falls over your neck. Don the baseball cap to hold the cloth in place. You're now protected front and back.

Pullover or stocking caps are favorites when the day cools down and evening draws near. An old northern Minnesota logger's axiom holds that "when your feet are cold, put on a hat," as an estimated 70 percent of body heat escapes through the head. These hats tend to fit snugly, which makes them handy in wind or when you're running across open water in a motorboat. Try them on for comfort before you buy—some designs fit the forehead comfortably but become too tight when pulled over the ears.

Footwear

Shoes, boots, and sandals have come a long way in their evolution to protect the feet of hikers and campers from the ground below. Years ago, serious hikers wore thick leather boots, with heavy grommets and laces so stout that you could almost use them for climbing rope, but today's products offer all the ankle support yet allow feet to breathe in hot weather or during times of intense exertion. The quest for strong, lightweight, breathable, and supportive materials continues, and the market is flooded with innovative designs. Low-cut trail shoes combine the aggressive lugs of traditional hiking boots with superlight uppers to give you sufficient ankle support but at a fraction of the weight. Sandals too have morphed to include aggressive treads and increased support above the ankles yet remain open to allow for plenty of airflow around the feet. You can still find plastic flip-flops for shower facilities or the beach, but with the right combination of supportive sandals and socks, you can have it all: Hike the trails of steep canyons by day, wade in the cool waters of a lake in the evening, then set your sandals outside the tent (unless you're in an area where porcupines or other salt-loving creatures might wander off with them); they'll be dry by morning.

Sock materials for campers include cotton, wool, polyester combinations, and neoprene. Choose cotton for coolness and durability, wool or the polyester combinations for comfort and wicking qualities on long hikes, and neoprene for wading or walking in winter's cold water or snow. In each material category you'll find high-top versions, low-cut versions, and a wide variety of weaves and thicknesses. In recent years, manufacturers have made sports socks with increased choices in patterns and colors. You'll want to do a bit of homework to determine what's best for you in terms of preventing blisters on long hikes. If possible, take socks for a half-hour "test drive" inside your shoes or sandals. If that's not an option and you're gearing up for a trip, purchase a few different types of socks. At the end of a long week of hiking and camping, one of them will emerge as your favorite.

Extras

Gloves are a must around the campfire. Leather remains the favorite for durability with handling firewood and other rough material, while thick cotton gloves are cheaper and protect the hands while doing all but the most intense camp chores. The duty of gloves often extends beyond fitting the hands—they can be doubled up for impromptu pot holders or for grabbing foil dinners from the fire. If you plan to cook on an open fire with a cast-iron frying pan or Dutch oven, you'll love a pair of heavy leather welding gloves. You can literally reach into the flames to extract the lids of cook pots, utensils, and other items.

Wool glove-and-mitten combos allow you to peel back the outer layer for increased dexterity.

Lightweight polyester weaves work well for protecting the hands from moisture and wind, but keep them away from hot surfaces or flames; they can melt into your skin. Woolen gloves are yet another choice, and might become your favorites for hiking in springtime or autumn when you expect to encounter fresh snow. Finger glove versions fit comfortably for most seasons, and look for mitten-glove combinations that allow you to undo a snap or Velcro and flip back the portion of the mitten that covers the fingers, exposing your fingers when you need extra dexterity for tasks such as tying knots or your shoes. The mitten-gloves have been available in wool for years, and neoprene versions have now hit the market.

DUFFEL BAGS AND BACKPACKS

Choosing a duffel bag to contain the aforementioned elements of shelter, especially clothing, requires a bit of thought: How big? Packing several pairs of pants, socks, underwear, midweight clothing, and outerwear for a weeklong outing

Waterproof duffel bags keep clothing and other supplies dry. Some come with straps that allow you to wear them like a frameless backpack.

requires a bag size of at least 40 cubic liters. Toss in your shower kit and other personal items, and 60 cubic liters might be closer to reality. The other option is to apportion your camping gear into parcels and arrange it in a few smaller duffel bags, which would be less cumbersome when loading and unloading the car. Some duffel bags have side compartments or inner partitions to help organize your goods. You'll find them in nylon and other synthetic materials, cotton, rubberized fabric, and waterproof cotton. When shopping for duffel bags, pay attention to the construction and quality of the zippers, buckles, and the stitching where the handles or straps join the main compartment of the bag. Other features of the duffel bag may include compression straps, which allow you to load the bag with compressible clothing and other soft goods, then cinch down the straps to drive out the air and drastically reduce volume—but not weight.

The beauty of a backpack is being able to arrange your entire camp in a single, ready-to-go bag that fits comfortably on your back. Though most backpacks have been designed with the overland hiker in mind, they often double as duffel bags on other outings. Unlike most duffel bags, backpacks have a wide assortment of easily accessible side compartments and additional chambers integrated within the top flap. Larger backpacks often include a zippered partition across the bottom third of the bag, providing a separate compartment for your sleeping bag. The remainder of your clothing, dehydrated food, trail snacks, and some toiletries fill the remaining section; hat, gloves, sunglasses, sunscreen, and other items fill the top or side compartments. Many backpacks also include external straps for bulky, lightweight items, such as sleeping pads or tarps.

If you plan a backpack camping trip, the total weight and bulk of your supplies is paramount. Besides knowing your physical abilities and how much weight you can safely and comfortably wear on your back, there is the question of bulk. If you're new to this type of camping, before you buy your first backpack, lay out all your food, clothing, and other necessary supplies across the living room floor. This will help you determine what you absolutely need to pack and what you can afford to leave behind. As you itemize your shelter and food, you'll quickly get an idea of how many cubic liters ("cubes") you'll need. Most campers end up with backpacks in the neighborhood of 60 cubic liters or more, while minimalists can squeeze everything into packs of around 40 cubic liters.

Among other important considerations in choosing the right backpack, check for adjustability in the distance between the arm straps and the belly strap. Taller campers often have longer torsos and will need more distance between the shoulder and waist straps; the opposite proves true for shorter campers. Most manufacturers include detailed instructions within one of the backpack pockets, with diagrams showing how to adjust internal straps to fit the torso.

Before you buy, commit to a detailed inspection. Backpacks have many straps, buckles, zippers, and stitches. Start at the top of the backpack and work your way down, following each seam and each strap to its end. Carefully look for cracked plastic buckles. Cracks in the female ends are extremely hard to see, and often you don't know they're cracked until you snap them together. Try them out—and listen: A cracked buckle or other fastener will often make a distinctly different sound than a good one. Time on the trail will wear buckles and stitching, so it's important to start with a sound backpack at the time of purchase.

The biggest killer of those plastic buckles? Slamming them in a car door. That's how I've broken all mine through the years. The fix? Snap the chest and waist straps back together when you're ready to load your backpack into a car or other vehicle. If you're flying with a backpack as luggage, most agents at airline ticket counters will remind you to buckle and cinch all your straps tightly together.

Properly Packing a Backpack

When it comes to loading the backpack for your trip, stuff the heaviest items in the bottom of your pack. Most tents and many sleeping bags will be the heaviest items in your mix of gear for long hikes and outdoor overnighting. Heavy items packed too high in the pack will rock from side to side as you stride and stress vertebrae and back muscles. Food (depending on your choice of entrees and snacks), your cookstove, and fuel sometimes approximate the weight of your sleeping bag. When deciding where to place items of equal weight, accessibility becomes a factor. You won't need the sleeping bag until nightfall, but you'll likely need food before that. Packing the food above the sleeping bag means unpacking contents from within the deeper reaches of your backpack just to get to a snack.

Given their density and shape, containers of stove fuel are best relegated to lower, external backpack compartments or pouches. White gas weighs approximately 7 pounds per gallon. Water weighs in at 8 pounds per gallon, which makes water bottles prime candidates for the lower pouches too.

Glass of any kind brings disproportionately heavy weight to the backpack. While it's easy enough to transfer goods to thin plastic containers (think reusing plastic bottles) to lighten your load, binoculars and camera lenses present an added challenge. The trick with glass is to keep it low yet easily accessible. Some backpacks integrate capacious front and side compartments within the waist strap, but if you've set your sights on a backpack that fits every other criterion but doesn't have external waist pouches, look for accessory pouches that snap or buckle on.

 CHARLIE GOES CAMPING

Backpacking is by far my favorite form of spending nights outdoors. A good part of the peak experience lies with hiking into the country and feeling the contrivances of civilization fall behind with each passing mile. But the nights out, away from established campgrounds and the proximity of vehicles, also hold an immense sense of adventure. Sunsets cleanse the clutter I've allowed to build up in my mind for months. Sleep comes intermittently throughout the night. I sometimes wake every hour and lie there for a few minutes, adjusting myself in the context of the place and its darkness before I drift back to sleep. It's a far cry from insomnia. My sporadic sleep patterns allow me to revisit something primordial in my hardwiring, and I love to let my imagination race to imagery of fur-clad ancestors, curled up in a mammoth skin for protection from the wind at night, waking often, senses keen for predators and the surrounding natural environment. Camping allows us to be part of that, to feel it, to reconnect with a world from whence we came.

Rocks strategically placed at anchoring points of a tent can hold down your shelter through the storms.

CHAPTER 3

STAKES, ROCKS, TOGGLES, AND TREES

NOW THAT YOU'VE SELECTED your shelter, you need to figure out how to keep it from blowing away. Though most tents come with a set of stakes, we have found them to be grossly inadequate. Even sleepovers on the front lawn have been compromised when the slightest breeze came along and ripped the tiny metal or plastic stakes from the ground. Not to overwork the axiom that bigger is better, we learned through the years that the simple solution to staking down tents involved a quick trip to a lumberyard or building supply store to purchase relatively inexpensive 40-penny common nails. Yep; they're huge. And they're heavy, especially if you follow our recommendation to purchase at least a dozen of them. Though these large nails can be driven into the ground with rocks, we prefer to use a hammer or the backside of a Hudson Bay axe or hatchet. And we drive them almost all the way in so their heads are nearly flush with the ground to prevent tripping over them and to protect summer toes in sandals.

Driving stakes increases motor skills in youths. They find accomplishment in driving the large pegs into the ground and securing the tent in wind.

The large nails have sufficient length to keep them anchored in beach sand and most soft soils, and they go unscathed when you drive them into mixed gravel and even coarse rock. We've even had great luck driving them into frozen ground. While it's true that the harder they go in, the harder they will be to extract, we have tricks for that part of the operation just ahead.

When staking out your tent, spread the corners to establish the footprint of the floor, place one of the nails into a loop, and give it a 360-degree twist before driving it in. This puts a twist in the tent loop, which grips the shank of the nail and lessens chances that the loop will slip past the head of the nail in gusty winds. The twist also prevents the tent loop from chafing in gusty winds. After you've staked out the corners and all the other loops along the perimeter of the tent, do the same for your guylines. There. That should hold down the tent in anything short of a hurricane.

To remove the stakes, gently tap the heads of the large spikes side to side from several different angles. This should elongate the deep holes and loosen the stakes enough to allow you to extract them with ease. To remove the spikes from frozen ground, drive them deeper into the ground, but only by a fraction of an inch. That breaks the bond of the frozen ground with the spikes, and they should pull out with ease.

Okay, so 40-penny nails are too heavy for a family backpacking trip. Smaller nails in the bins still beat the stakes that come with most tents in terms of keeping the corners secure.

FASTENERS

As a slight compromise in sheer holding power, but much lighter in weight, the construction market has made great strides in developing fasteners, particularly those used in building outdoor porches and patio furniture. They come in sizes up to several inches long, and their aggressive screw ends are self-starting in most materials, especially wood. These fasteners—hybrids between screws and bolts—can be driven into some soils and screwed into cracks within rocks, the

The orange plastic twist-in fasteners weigh a fraction of huge steel spikes. You can twist them in with your hands.

roots of trees, or other solid substrates to keep your tent tied down. These are a bit more complicated in that they require a small socket wrench to screw them into harder ground. My personal camping gear includes a socket (⁵⁄₁₆-inch) that fits the heads of the bolts and a small ¼-inch-drive ratchet setup that makes screwing and unscrewing the fasteners quick and easy.

TOGGLES

In some conditions, such as deep snow, mud, or soft sand, large nails and screws cannot grab well enough to hold down the tent. In these situations, nails can be inserted into tent loops halfway, then twisted so that they act like a toggle, flat on the ground. The trick is to find rocks or other rubble to set on top of the toggle to keep it secure. The more weight, the better. Sometimes I forgo the nails in favor of a longer stick that can span the distance between two tent loops and then anchor those down with larger chunks of wood, rocks, or both. For sand

Flat branches laid flat with rocks on top create a trusted anchoring system for your tent when metal stakes add too much weight to your camping equation.

and snow, I often dig a trench of up to a foot deep, insert the toggle through the tent loop, drop it into the trench, and bury it.

TREES

Most tents come with guy outs, small loops of webbing sewn into the seams of the tent's rainfly, halfway between the ground and the peak. Manufacturers usually supply a set of guylines in a small packet with the newly purchased tent, but I rarely use those as they are too short. I opt instead for fluorescent green parachute cord or sections of mountain climbing accessory cord. I like to tie 10 to 12 feet of the cord onto each guy loop on the rainfly and consider that an integral part of the tent. The extra length has come in handy countless times over the years when I've been able to reach a nearby root, shrub, or tree to secure the tent. Though guylines can't always perform the duty of ground stakes at the floor of the tent, they do fortify the tent in wind. I chose fluorescent green cord for the guylines so that they show up better in low light. Guylines can also serve as clotheslines to dry out bathing suits or other wet clothing after a swim.

Note: When considering trees to use for guylines, the ends of tarps, or pitching a hammock, check out the tops to make sure the trees are healthy. Also, look for large dead limbs overhead. These can kill you if they suddenly snap and fall.

Many tents have loops or rings that allow you to connect their tarps to trees. We use climbing accessory cord to anchor the tent; doubling it doesn't hurt the bark of trees.

CHARLIE GOES CAMPING

As a family, much of a successful camping experience depends on problem solving. The accomplishments of learning the correct knots, scoping out a safe camping area, and pitching a tent or creating a structure to endure wind and rain often morph into a game. When I was 16, my brothers, Chris (15) and Matt (8), and I would often camp with friends. We grew up with plenty of quality time in the woods and relished weekend trips when we could catch fish, cook them up, and then sleep out on the shore of a distant lake.

I was into canoes back then, and one of my favorite campouts ever was when we hauled my 17-footer out of the lake and inverted it, propping one end up over a downed tree. I crawled under it for shelter with just a sleeping bag and a pad. It began to drizzle that night, but I stayed warm and dry, falling asleep to the raindrops sputtering against the canoe's aluminum hull.

Hot chicken stew is ready to serve from a Dutch oven.

EAT

Food is to the camper as fuel is to the vehicle to get you there—but with the added duty that it must provide body heat. That last factor can sneak up on you as a camper, unless your daily routine at home involves hiking and other strenuous activities then sleeping out in the relative chill of the night. Even in many deserts, nightfall brings a sharp dip in the ambient air temperature and forces the body to metabolize extra calories to maintain that 98.6°F we have all come to consider normal.

The following chapters offer a step-by-step guide on how to prepare and care for food that will not only keep you healthy and warm but also add an extra dimension to your family camping experience. In nearly all cultures, food is associated with festivities and other events as a catalyst that draws folks together, but eating enters a realm of its own in the great outdoors.

Water is everything on an
extended camping trip.

CHAPTER 4

WATER

WATER, THAT ESSENTIAL LIQUID OF LIFE, weighs in at 8 pounds a gallon, and I didn't want to pack another 16 pounds of it on my back, even though I knew I'd need at least that much for a few days in the backcountry. I was standing at the counter of an outdoor gear supply store. In my left hand I held a small ceramic purifying filter, capable of producing 30 cubic centimeters of potable water with each stroke of its tiny plastic pump handle. Meanwhile, my right hand was having an anxiety attack as it fished for the wallet in my pocket—the price of the contraption was right at a $100 bill.

Therein lies every camper's dilemma when it comes to safe water: Pack it or make it. We use an old rule of thumb when we're teaching survival classes. The human body can last:

Three minutes without air;

Three days without water;

Three weeks without food.

That three-part rule rides on the assumptions that said human body is not fighting harsh weather, not performing strenuous exercise, or not exposed to other conditions that can drastically reduce those times. The rule also doesn't consider that, even if you have ample food, you still need water for the metabolism required to create body heat and move muscles.

Depending on your camping plans, water requirements should top the list. Many campgrounds have sources of clean water, but some don't, and in remote settings you'll need to provide for yourself. You can buy water bottled, by the case, or in larger containers. Or you can recycle, filling plastic containers that previously contained soft drinks with water right from your tap. By conservative estimates, I figure 1 gallon per person per day, and that's not counting water for washing or other needs. If you plan to pack your water, it's fairly simple to do the math.

WATER SOURCES

If you're studying a topographic map and calculating the distances between lakes, rivers, or streams, the hydration situation becomes complicated, especially if you plan to camp in unfamiliar territory. Though those squiggly lines representing creeks and other waterways have been mapped out in an inviting blue ink, the water in some of those drainages may be brown and teeming with insect larvae and fecal matter from beavers, otters, ducks, deer, and other wildlife (and possibly humans). A dose of the wrong critter crap in your cup could mean scuttling your trip and perhaps taking weeks or even months to recover.

The safety net between you and a mess of gastrointestinal setbacks lies in a proper approach to filtering your water. As an alternative to filtering, some campers prefer "dropping" their drinking water with doses of iodine or other purification tablets. With the luxury of a camp stove or other source of heat and a suitable container, boiling is another option.

In any of these scenarios, locating the best source of water is the key. Just about every creek I've encountered varies in gradience and velocity of flow, and small tributaries or freshets that feed into the mainstream often prove even safer. Years ago, I had crossed over a mountain pass. As I dropped downhill into a broad valley, I felt my legs wanting to cramp and a slight dizziness, the early signs of dehydration. Though I'd traveled along the shore of a swift-moving river for more than half an hour, this particular body of water was inundated with spawning salmon. I had the latest and greatest in purification filters (yeah, I plunked down that $100), but the stench of decaying flesh and the color of the water seemed too risky.

Finally I spotted a tiny feeder creek emanating from a crack in the bedrock of a steep cliff to my right. Clearly no salmon had swum in this water. The creek was cold and clear but ran at a trickle, so I spent some time finding a small pool in which to insert the intake end of the filter. The little pump did its magic, and soon I was back on the trail toward my destination—and rehydration.

During a four-day trip with a volunteer trail crew one summer, we camped in a series of long ridges between the mountains and couldn't find a source of water that wasn't infested with mosquito larvae. There were six of us, and we needed a minimum of 8 gallons per day. The only source of water within miles of where we needed to camp was a pool the size of a Hula-Hoop in diameter, only 3 inches deep, full of sediment, and fed by a trickle of water no thicker than my pinky finger. As a group we took turns carefully dipping small containers into the shallow pool so that we wouldn't disturb the sediment. We eventually filled a

High alpine streams tend to carry fewer impurities than slow-moving water at lower elevations. Still, filtering is in order to ensure safety.

3-gallon bucket, which had had been rigged with three ceramic filters mounted on its bottom. The bucket containing the filters nested near the top of another bucket, and what trickled down through the hours would be our drinking water. Filling the bucket each morning and each night, we maintained hydration and nobody got sick.

Filtering

Though pump-operated filtering systems still exist, today's camper has several other choices, including drinking straws, water bottle caps, and other designs that incorporate filters internally and allow you to make drinking water as you need it. These devices tend to produce far less volume and have trouble keeping up with the demands of multiple users. Some systems involve two bags containing up to 5 liters each. You fill the input bag, hang it from a limb, then open a filtering valve on the hose that runs between the two bags. The water runs from the input bag through a hose that contains and inline filter, and by morning you have 5 liters of potable water.

As a precursor to treating water when sediment or other solids are present in the source, use a bandana or the cleanest fabric of a lightweight shirt or other garment to filter out the larger particles. I have a silk shirt that strains water nicely, but paper towels or other materials make suitable strainers in a pinch.

Warm-water limestone streams like this one in Alabama can be used as a source of water but require filtering before drinking.

Boiling

With a sufficient camp stove or other source of heat and a suitable container, boiling water becomes a handy option for sterilization. Even then, it pays to look for the clearest source of water near your camp. In the case of that salmon stream, for instance, I'm not sure I could have put up with the taste. As for boiling times, the US Centers for Disease Control and Prevention recommend a rolling boil for 1 minute—3 minutes at altitudes higher than 6,562 feet (2,000 meters).

An alternative to boiling involves treatment with chlorine drops or tablets, iodine drops, or iodine-based tablets. A 3-ounce bottle can treat up to 2,000 liters of water. Manufacturers of the iodine products recommend 5 drops per quart when the source water is clear and 10 drops when the water is cloudy. Though dropping water for sterilization makes for lighter weight when packing through the backcountry, try it out at home first. You might not be able to tolerate the taste of iodine; even worse, you might have an allergic reaction. I have used dropping several times in the backcountry when it was the only option, and the bottles are handy at home in case city water systems become compromised from hurricanes, earthquakes, fires, or other natural calamities.

Killing the Bad Stuff

The stuff in the source water that affects your gastrointestinal health includes giardia, *Vibrio cholerae* (bacterium that causes cholera), *E. coli*, and salmonella. The trick to iodine or chlorine drops or tablets is to wait for at least 30 minutes for the chemicals to kill the critters, and the treatment works best if water is at room temperature or above. Only after the water has been treated for a sufficient time can you can add flavorings to counteract the taste of iodine or chlorine. Common additions include lemon or lime drops, powdered electrolytes, and other drink mixes.

Campers who can't or don't want to boil their water often use iodine or chlorine drops or tablets to purify their water.

A situation that rules out filtering or dropping as a solution comes with camping near large cities or in other areas where surface waters have been contaminated by industrial or agricultural pollution. You can filter out or kill organisms to purify water, but you can't remove toxins such as metals, acids, and other chemical pollutants.

CATCHMENT

There's another, intriguing and fun way for campers to procure their drinking water, provided it rains: catchment. Nomadic animal herders in arid regions of the world have learned to capture enough water from intermittent downpours to meet the needs of large herds of cattle, horses, and sheep. Catchment, in the scale needed to water the herds, involves a broad apron-shaped trough that funnels down to a narrow trough that feeds into a pipe on its downhill end. During infrequent but significant rainstorms, large amounts of water run from the collection apron into underground cisterns, where the darkness and cool ground prevent evaporation. The ranchers have devised a way to pump the water out to meet their animals' needs.

The underlying idea behind catchment is to grab huge amounts of water during infrequent rainstorms in arid areas and store it for use during dry periods. The trick to catching enough rainwater to meet the needs of cattle—or a large family or group—depends on the size of the device and the system to contain the water. In the campers' world, a clean tarp, free of chemicals such as fire retardant or waterproofing, strung up in the branches of a tree and shaped to funnel water to its downhill end can produce gallons of potable water in minutes during severe rainstorms. Years ago I read articles about spreading a tarp by its four corners among trees and puncturing a hole in its center so that water would flow naturally downhill and fall through the hole to a container below. But I couldn't get past the idea of putting a hole in one of my new tarps and came up with the alternative rig described above.

Though catchment is only as dependable as the rainstorms in some areas of the country, it's a safe bet in other areas, such as southeast and south-central Alaska from August through October. In any case, catchment provides great fun as a peripheral activity on longer trips. Even with your primary source of safe drinking water secured, the water funneled off the end of a tarp into every possible container in camp provides a bonus for bathing and rinsing out soiled or sweat-riddled clothing.

Solar Still

Yet another method of cleansing water relies on a little do-it-yourselfer knowledge or purchasing a refined version of a cool contraption known as the solar still. Hint to parents: Kids love this! What the solar still lacks in timely production of drinking water, it more than makes up for in entertainment value and demonstrating the earth's water cycle. You can make one by joining two plastic soft drink bottles together at their necks, using adapters or conjoining them with a few rounds of electrical tape. Fill one of the bottles with your unfiltered, "dirty" water, screw on the empty bottle to form the still's top, prop it up at a slight incline, and let the sun do its work. In time the sun evaporates water molecules off the top of the unfiltered water in the bottom bottle. The evaporated water leaves the junk behind and forms dew in the chamber of the upper bottle. When the air becomes saturated and can't hold its moisture any longer, it "rains" into the recesses in the upper bottle, where it can be poured off as potable drinking water. The process is slow (although multiple units increase production), but it is fun to watch and a great science project for homeschoolers.

Few experiences can equal the warmth of a campfire and a riotous display of the northern lights.

CHAPTER 5

FIRE

IS THERE ANY OTHER element that delivers us further from our fears of the dark and satisfies our need to maintain body temperature more than fire? Sure, many of us had to read and regurgitate Jack London's classic "To Build a Fire" to teachers in our seventh-grade English Lit classes; but seriously, what do we need to know about building a fire in our various camping situations?

We need air, a fuel supply—and a spark.

It all sounds simple enough, but inadequacies in either of the last two elements will leave us "cold camping" throughout our trip. Spark is the critical component in making a successful fire with the wide selection of fuels and camp stoves available on the market, but if our camping plans turn decidedly rustic and involves wood—and the moisture content of that wood rises much above 20 percent—all the spark in the world won't make it burn.

WOOD

Good stuff when we can find it, great stuff when it's cured, firewood remains the fuel that links us to our primordial pasts. We gather to socialize around the campfire's glow and sit close to its flames, instinctive behaviors to savor fire's ambient warmth. Its light flickers upon our faces against a backdrop of pitch

Purchase dried firewood by the bundle at convenience stores near camping areas. Some campgrounds offer dry firewood for sale.

black, isolates us as subjects against nothingness, and empowers us to conjure up stories of ghosts and ghoulish creatures or recitations of literature that would seem out of place anywhere else. We will endure its smoke in our eyes; put up with blackened cook pots, smudged clothing, and melted utensils; and return home with our hair reeking—only to relish and plan when we get to go camping and do it all over again.

When considering campfire wood, it helps to know a bit about tree species and some of the characteristics of the fuel each provides. Trees fall into two basic groups: coniferous—species bearing cones for seed and adorned with needles instead of leaves—and deciduous trees. Deciduous trees can be defined by broad green leaves in their living state. Though they resemble one another somewhat in foliage, densities of the wood vary widely among these species. Aspen, a key tree in the making of paper, cottonwood, willow, and alder are soft woods that lend themselves to whittling, making marshmallow-roasting sticks, and other campfire fun. Trees with softer wood are often full of sticky sap in summer when the leaves are green. Using aspen or other soft deciduous species for firewood requires that the trees have been cut and dried ahead of time, which can take the better part of a year.

Firewood from these trees burns readily when dry, but the soft wood burns more quickly than firewood made from hardwoods. Firewood from oak, hickory, birch, cherry, maple, and some subspecies of ash may take longer to cure than the softwoods—and starting a fire with kindling made from these species takes longer than with softwoods—but they burn much longer and provide a great bed of glowing coals for cooking. The residual heat and abundance of coals hidden beneath the ash go a long way toward rejuvenating the campfire the next morning.

Coniferous species such as pine, spruce, fir, and larch are usually softer than hardwoods, but their sap contains resin, which has a sharp, solvent-like scent. The other unique characteristic of coniferous firewood is that it crackles and pops louder than firewood made from other tree species. Though the crackling adds aesthetic appeal to the camping experience, coniferous firewood often tosses glowing embers into the air. What goes up must come down, and depending on where they land, the red-hot embers can burn holes through tent flies and other nearby camping equipment. Another drawback to firewood from pine or other resinous woods is that it can impart a turpentine-like taste to food cooked over its coals.

Firewood from coniferous trees also needs curing, and curing means cutting and drying wood well ahead of time. In campgrounds where burning is permitted, campers can often buy firewood. Local convenience stores near popular camping areas may also offer wood wrapped in bundles. We've seen bundles of split wood containing mixtures of coniferous and deciduous hardwoods.

Note: National parks and forests and many states prohibit bringing in firewood from other areas, which can spread disease and insect pests.

TINDER

Now for the Jack London part. To build a fire, you have to start small. And you have to start dry—very dry. We're talking the lint from your dryer and tiny twigs or wood shavings here. We use a lot of wood in our camping expeditions up here in Alaska, and if that's not enough—more nights than not, even in summer—we have a fire going in our woodstove to alleviate the evening chill. Working with firewood year-round gives us lots of small scraps, twigs, dry birch bark (like paper) chips, and sawdust to pack along as fire starter.

Years ago, a friend introduced me to the art of making swizzle sticks. No, not the little plastic

You can purchase self-contained fire-starter kits that include sparking devices and flammable paste.

CHARLIE GOES CAMPING

I remember checking out countless books about camping and wood lore from the school library when I was 13. One image that sticks with me yet is a gorgeous set of ink-like drawings in a book (I can't remember the title.) in which the artist drew round logs of firewood arranged in various configurations ranging from upright and conical, like a miniature tepee frame, to a triangular stack lying flat on the ground. The text below each drawing described the merits of stacking the wood this way or that, but the one that caught my eye had been labeled in a cursive cutline: "Hunter's Fire."

In my adolescent days of self-discovery, that picture of the hunter's fire got to me. In the background, a rugged bearded man squatted on his heels, arms outstretched, palms open to accept the fire's warmth like some great gift. I wanted to be that man. Still do. The supportive text explained that by stacking the logs in a pattern with three logs on the bottom, laying two on top of that layer and then a single log on top, each round log had limited air available to it and thus would not burn up too fast, allowing said rugged hunter longer lasting comfort.

It looked so cool.

Soon enough, I was out in the woods again, on one of Minnesota's deep-winter afternoons. I found what looked like a downed dry birch and sawed it into logs with a small handsaw I always packed along. I kindled the fire using some of the dry bark, laid dry twigs upon branches, and added more branches until I had a roaring fire and a burgeoning bed of coals. When I thought the fire was hot enough, I piled on the logs and arranged them just like I saw in the book. A half hour later, my eyes had teared—and those tears were freezing to the cuff of my army-surplus parka. I was cold, and that fire did nothing but produce smoke. I have tried the log arrangement several times since then, but always with limited success. Campfires need air, and a haphazard approach to heaping firewood onto a blaze often provides the best airflow from bottom to top.

thingies used to stir drinks at a bar; but with his excellent knife skills and a dry branch of wood, he taught me to mimic their decorative tops by shaving tassels of wood into tight curls These are small enough that I can crowd a half dozen into a small plastic sandwich bag.

Many convenience stores sell artificial logs made of compressed sawdust, wax, or other fuel source. You can forgo the kindling process with these, as they can be lit with just a match.

Other Fuels

If the campground or other recreational area doesn't permit campfires, another option is a camp stove. These efficient stoves range from tiny burners that screw onto small disposable propane tanks to large, two-burner models that run on white gas, or "camp fuel," as it is often labeled. Other camp stoves use a combination of butane, propane, and other fuels to light up instantly and bring a liter of water to a boil in mere minutes. You'll find white gas/camp fuel in cans on the shelves of outdoors stores.

Most stoves using camp fuel rely on a process known as generation, which involves pumping up their tanks with a small plunger pump, opening the fuel valve to allow a few drops of fuel in a pan, lighting the stove with the valve shut

Blends of propane and butane fuels make tiny stoves roar, and boiling water is only moments away at any altitude.

off, and letting the residual fuel heat a coiled tube. As the tube heats under the flame, the fuel within begins to boil; when the fuel is hot enough, you light the main burner. These little stoves roar delightfully when they're cranked up. They have been a favorite among winter campers for years, as they will light at 20 below zero, when propane and other fuels will not.

Meager daylight hours and the rainy season are factors in many of our back-country trips, meaning that time and dry wood are in short supply. Though the conditions dash our chances of a campfire, we manage a similar aesthetic by arranging stones and placing our tiny stoves within them. The stones gather peripheral heat over time, serving as pot warmers and great places to dry out wet gloves and socks.

Those stones under and around the camp stoves also come into play when the country has been dry and fire danger is running moderate to high. One spark lofted from a campfire is all it takes to start a major forest fire.

Note: Check regional and local laws and restrictions to find out if camp stoves are allowed before heading out on your trip.

SPARK

We have ignition! Like the crackling voices of spaceflight crews to Ground Control, you've got to have a suitable spark to get the good times rolling. The more volatile the fuel, the less intense the spark has to be to ignite a fire.

Camping equipment manufactures offer no shortage of piston-powered fire starters. With these fire starters, you insert a chunk of charcoal or a small wad of charcoal cloth into a small metal receptacle centered inside the top of a metal rod that protrudes several inches from a comfortable wooden or plastic handle. With the coal seated in the chamber, the other half of the handle nests over the top and telescopes so that the two halves slide together. The two halves fit together so snugly that when you slam them shut, the temperature of the air compressed between them rises several hundred degrees and ignites the charcoal to produce a glowing ember that is smaller than a ladybug. Extracting the tiny ember from the receptacle and dropping it into a swatch of clothes dryer lint or other combustible material is only the first step in building a fire. In many instances, the lint may be nested within a tinder bundle consisting of a softball-size aggregation of fine wood shavings, paper, grasses, and other materials; and you may have to hold it in gloved hands close to your face and exhale with just the right vigor to blow the fire to life. If you produce only a smoky smudge in your first attempts, keep trying. You'll get it—and the satisfaction is immense.

CHARLIE GOES CAMPING

As a kid, I read stories of yore, when the mountain men of the West started a fire by rolling their hands back and forth rapidly along a dowel-shaped twig of softwood so that it spun like a drill. They held the twig vertically, putting their weight into it so that its tip generated heat as it bored into yet softer wood that formed a base plate. I tried the hand-drill method many times and never raised the temperature of the wood much higher than the 98.6°F of my sweaty hands. In time I came to regard starting fires with hand and bow drills as theory and lumped their authenticity in with the "hunter's fire."

Even more mythical were stories of how these fierce outdoor heroes would grab the perfect ember from the fire they'd created from scratch with their drills, embed it in fine sand or dust, and store it within a small leather pouch they wore around their necks. They'd nurse that ember throughout the day, checking to make sure it had sufficient air to keep it smoldering with enough heat and glow to start the next fire down the line. If the ember method failed, it meant going back to the drill.

Cool stuff to think about, but the romance quickly disappears when you've caught a chill and need to get a campfire or a camp stove blazing away as quickly as possible.

There are countless internet videos about how to use—even build—these cool contraptions. With practice, they become very effective fire starters.

For a little less primitive means of sparking a fire to life, consider magnesium flint starters. These small units consist of a comfortable handle that supports a magnesium rod alongside a smaller flint rod. Affixed to the handle by thin twine or a leather thong, you'll find a small flat piece of steel with sharp edges that will allow you to scrape shavings of magnesium off the rod into a loose pile within your lint or other tinder. When you have a sufficient pile of the bright silver shavings, point the fire-starting tool close to the shavings and slide the same steel over the flint rod to produce a series of sparks. Magnesium burns blindingly bright and will produce a flash much hotter than the glowing ember described earlier. The downside is that the flash will last only a second or two in comparison to a glowing ember. If you've laid your tinder out correctly, however, you're well on your way to a blaze.

If you're having trouble choosing between a piston-style fire starter or a magnesium flint starter, the easy answer is to acquire both. Nothing brings greater reward than mastering a skill, and the experience is accentuated when we watch our children succeed at these outdoor challenges. If nothing else, pack these tools along for nightly campsite entertainment.

Fire starters are to igniting wood as lighters, strikers, and matches are to lighting camp stoves. Because a steady supply of gas flows through the stove with the opening of the supply valve, modern fuels alleviate the need for tinder. Still, sufficient spark is the genesis of any of your cooking or heating endeavors.

Sit back, listen to the crackling of the fire, and forget the fast-paced world you left behind. You're camping!

Butane Lighters

Butane lighters have remained a favorite fire starter through the years, with strike-anywhere matches following close behind. Both fire starters are inexpensive. Lighter multipacks are readily available at most gas stations and convenience stores; outdoor supply and camping stores carry waterproof strike-anywhere matches. Store them in the smaller pouches of your backpack or fanny pack.

Keeping lighters close to the body is paramount in the Pacific Northwest and here in Alaska during fall and winter, when incessant rains fall or temperatures drop below freezing. A wet or cold lighter often becomes useless; even though they might throw a spark or two, you may have to warm them up near your body for more than an hour before they throw sufficient flame to light your campfire or stoves.

Butane lighters are compact; however, they sometimes come up short when reaching into the recesses to light barbecue grills, candles cradled within protective wind globes, or other situations that require a little extra length. Camping equipment manufacturers offer versions that range from several inches to nearly a foot long. These lighters have small triggers that are pulled to release a gas supply down their long tubes while the thumb operates a striker that ignites the butane. Originally designed to reach in deep to light gas- or wood-burning fireplaces, they've found new life around campsites.

Matches

You may find long-necked lighters' sulfur-burning counterparts, matches, nearly 10 inches in length. They work great for reaching between the grates of a propane barbecue grill to light the burner. No long-necked lighter? No long-stemmed matches? Never fear. You can extend regular wooden matches by using a small pliers, or your camp gear may include hemostats. These stainless wonders from the medical world can grip a match and light candle wicks or burners beneath grates or other protective shrouding. We'll get into the manifold uses of the hemostats in our chapter on camp hacks (see page 173).

You can light gas grills and other camp stoves where the main burner is highly accessible by using strikers. These are similar to the flint fire starters described earlier in this chapter, but they lack the magnesium rod and involve only the flint against the steel to produce a hot spark. These have worked particularly well for lighting multi-burner white gas stoves.

In the end, fire is what you make of it. As a family, it is endless fun to arrive at camp and explore the unique ways to bring light and heat to the outdoor experience. The hoarder in the family can savor a copious collection of dryer lint or other tinder materials. Who knows? There may be a family member who's bent on mastering the hand-drill method of fire starting. If that's the case, do not discourage.

CHARLIE GOES CAMPING

Decades after I'd dismissed the idea of hand drills as a viable method of starting fires, my friend Alan, who was at the time my supervisor in an outdoor leadership program, pulled me aside one afternoon with a gleam in his eye.

"Check this out," he said as he reached into a daypack and extracted a footlong branch of dried elderberry and a piece of soft wood resembling a birch conk (a fungus that grows on birch trees). Alan explained that he'd had success starting fires with drills elsewhere across the Lower 48 but had only recently discovered the combination of species and relative dryness of each required to make fire in Alaska. I watched in awe as he spun the drill in his hands, up and down, and blew into his tiny pile of tinder. It took him all of 45 seconds to impress me and less than 2 minutes to produce a hot coal within the tinder. He picked it up, blew life into the ember, and his tinder burst into flames. Extinguishing the tiny fire, he handed me his primitive tools as a gift. I have tried several times to start a blaze of my own with the drill. I try again each summer.

Someday.

Specialized camp cooking tools can bring s'mores and more into another dimension when you're preparing meals over a fire.

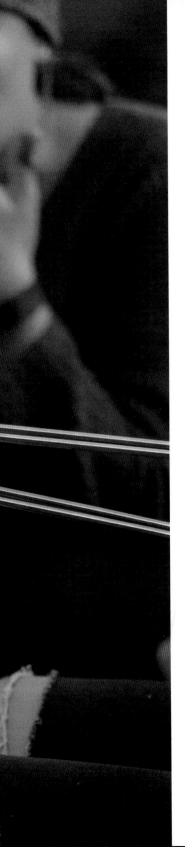

CHAPTER 6

POTS, PANS, AND UTENSILS

THE JIM PAN. It was an aluminum pan with a diameter of 6 inches and enough depth to hold almost a quart of water. It was lightweight with a lid that fit snugly, yet it had enough resilience that it retained its shape despite its frequent position under heavy stuff at the bottom of our packs or under a pile of heavy goods stacked in a wooden camp kit that spread the width of my aluminum canoe. Though it probably had some proprietary name denoting the company that made it, we came to know it affectionately as the Jim pan—an abbreviated form of the name that circumnavigated its side in indelible black marker: "Jim Lieberman."

Though we had no idea who he was, we found the Jim pan on a family camping trip while beachcombing the north shore of Lake Winnibigoshish in Minnesota. The rest of our family camping utensils were purchased at garage sales, and the Jim pan marked a significant step in our evolution from camping together as a family with large cast-iron frying pans and porcelain-coated steel coffeepots to camping with lightweight cooking gear of our own as my brother

Chris and I began pushing into the outdoors in ventures that eventually brought us to Alaska. In addition to the Jim pan, we purchased other ultralight cooking utensils as part of the gear we used for decades of camping in the mountains.

ACQUIRING YOUR CAMP COOK KIT

The years have rolled on. We've raised families of our own, and now we're camping with our grandchildren. From heavy cast-iron Dutch ovens to 3-ounce titanium cook pots to rolls of aluminum foil, we've got 'em all and use 'em all during various camping situations in the course of the year. To keep most camp utensils separated from our household renditions, we store them in a designated storage container. These plastic totes cost little and allow us to have a ready-to-go set of dishes, pots and pans, coffeepots, forks, knives, spoons, matches, dish soap, washbasins, dish towels, and can openers—a complete kit—whenever a family camping opportunity springs up.

Acquiring a designated set of camping utensils via garage sales constitutes family fun in itself. Pick a Saturday morning, load up the car, and enjoy the surprise of what you can buy for less than $20.

Pots

As for what comprises a camping utensil kit, group size and your mode of travel dictates what to pack. If camping means loading the kids into a vehicle with lots of room and motoring to a campground that allows campfires, a Dutch oven will eventually wind up in your kit. Sure, they're heavy; but load one up with anything from chili to ribs to soups or cornbread, bury it in hot coals, and taste its magic. The secret to the Dutch oven is that the thick cast iron disperses heat evenly through its bottom and sides. Many models have a lid that can be inverted to form a shallow dish where you can place hot coals on top for oven-like baking.

A Dutch oven purchased new will require some curing. Pour in a little olive oil or other cooking oil and heat the Dutch oven in a household oven, or bury it in campfire coals. In time the pot will turn from its original metallic gray to black. Washing the Dutch oven with water only (no soap) ensures that the cast iron will stay cured and free of rust.

Though Dutch ovens may be used to warm water or keep water warm near the edge of a campfire, it's hard to beat the versatility of a large aluminum or titanium kettle or a large metal teapot that holds at least a gallon of liquid. Camping life requires heating water for washing dishes, bathing, and making hot drinks, and these utensils are lightweight and heat water quickly on a campfire or burner of a camp stove. Some have heavy wire handles arching over their tops; others

Dutch ovens come in a variety of sizes and with dome-shaped or flat lids. Flat-topped models are better suited to piling coals on top for oven-like heat.

have rigid handles integral with their sides or rims. The beauty of the overhead handle comes into play when it's time to fetch water from a well or an outdoor faucet; the pot can be carried with one hand and swings freely, which spills less water. Some styles offer both types of handles.

A smaller pot that holds a quart to a quart and a half with a solid lid has been invaluable for cooking vegetables and soups and making pudding or other camp goodies. These can also be used to heat water for coffee, tea, or hot chocolate, but they shine for making hot cereal or warming canned soup or leftovers.

Whatever you choose, invest in a set of pot holders. Or buy a pair of heavy leather gloves that work as pot holders but also protect your hands when doing other camping chores, such as cutting or splitting firewood.

Coffeepots

Some folks can't function without coffee; some folks have to brew it a certain way. If percolation is the name of the game in your camp, it pays to buy a coffeepot designed just for that. French presses and other coffee-brewing contraptions can get by with water from a cook pot or teapot, but perked coffee requires the pot and its innards, which should include a base and hollow stem, an internal strainer with its own lid, and that make-or-break little glass bubble thingy that goes into the top. We have lost those little bubble thingies and had to plug the resulting hole with a wad of aluminum foil, but the pot loses nearly all functionality without one.

Pans

Frying pans. Plural. Cast iron can be hard to beat for many applications, but we also like several models and sizes of nonstick coated aluminum. The coated pans require a little extra care when it comes to cleaning and should not be scraped with metal spatulas or spoons or other materials that can scratch the coating. The cast-iron versions, like the Dutch oven, require curing if they're new. Dump in a few teaspoons of cooking oil, rub it along the bottom and sides of the pan, then put the pan on a burner to make it hot enough that the oil begins smoking. Remove the pan from the heat, let it cool, and wipe out the excess oil with paper towel (save for fire-starting materials). Your pan should be ready to fry fish or meat, sauté vegetables, and produce great camp meals.

Garage sales and secondhand stores are great places to acquire your camping dishes.

Dishes, Cups, and Utensils

Dishes, cups, saucers, and spoons and other silverware are perhaps the most fun to acquire at garage sales or secondhand stores. This is where family members get a chance to express themselves as individuals. You can buy just one cup or one plate, as pieces are likely missing from a complete set. The result is an eclectic, often colorful assortment of utensils that lie dormant in their plastic storage container and bring smiles when they come out again at camp.

Through the years, we've purchased an array of plastic dishes for their durability, light weight, and the added attribute that they don't take the edge off a sharp knife if you're carving up a steak or other cut of meat on them. The set of plastic plates we have of late actually came from my parents, and if memory serves me, they were part of an assortment we acquired for camping when we were kids and later used to outfit a hunting shack we built in northern Minnesota. We sold the shack and let go of the lease on the hunting property. But the dishes made their way to Alaska via Mom and Dad's camper when they lived with us for several weeks and were the key ingredient to building our first cabin.

We have an array of metal and plastic silverware. For Christmas and other occasions, we have received a goodly number of titanium forks and spoons. Our plastic forks and spoons, however, are not the disposable versions, which snap at the handle or leave one of their skinny plastic tines embedded in a pot roast. We bought these at an outdoor camping gear store, and they are cheap. We've also inherited some camping utensils from mix-ups with friends and have several brightly colored "sporks"—a spoon on one end and a fork on the other.

With the exception of butter knives, the knives we take camping stay sharp—razor sharp. For years we carried serrated steak knives, but they grew so dull we retired them and went back to straight-bladed models. We are hunters and fishers and as such are never far from a sharpening stone. Besides safety, proper knife storage ensures that they'll stay sharp. We've wrapped them, isolated from one another, in leather, cardboard, newspaper, or fabric and then stuffed them into a plastic drinking glass.

When it comes to storing butter knives, forks, spoons, a small kitchen thermometer, and a few other camp kitchen accoutrements, it would be hard to beat an invention that Cheryl came up with years ago. Is there a seamstress in your family? This handy utensil holder has been sewn with an extended flap and several long compartments for various silverware and a side pocket for spices, plastic pot scrapers, and miniature can openers. We insert the utensils into their respective sleeves, double the flap over their tops, roll the whole works up tightly, and tie it up with integral straps. It holds enough utensils for four campers.

There are can openers that work and those that don't, but somehow they end up at garage sales or in our kitchen drawers at home. Try before you buy to make sure they work, and as a backup, pack several military-issued mini openers. You may have heard them called "galloping Girdies" or "P-38s," but they are small, lightweight, and can open even large cans in less than a minute.

Other handy items to add to your camp kit could include spatulas, tongs, screen filters, coffee funnels and paper filters, long-handled serving spoons, a small cutting board (we have both plastic and wood), shish-kabob skewers in either metal or bamboo, dish soap, a metallic scouring pad, dish towels, a tablecloth, and trash bags. Somewhere along the line when our children were small, we spilled a small assortment of grilling spices and black pepper in our plastic camping tote. Though we cleaned it out then and have cleaned it many times since, every time we lift off the lid, the aroma of those spices wafts out and conjures up fond memories of when were younger and camping with our precious little family.

Washbasins are a must. Buy at least two, maybe even three, of the same style so that they nest. These work great for washing and rinsing dishes, and you can relegate one of them to personal hygiene. Some come in different colors, which makes it easy to differentiate between kitchen and bathing chores. If different colors aren't an option, you can label each with an indelible marker. Many campers we know don't care and use the same basins for dishes and washing their hair.

COOLERS

All the prep done at home for great outdoor meals can vanish in a matter of hours if certain foods aren't kept at temperatures between 35°F and 40°F. Meat, eggs, cheese and other dairy products, and anything containing mayonnaise can turn deadly with bacteria as the hot sun beats down on your car while you're off on a hike.

The solution for maintaining personal safety and good eats is to add the coolest of coolers to your camp set. When it comes to shopping for the perfect cooler, start with choosing the right size. Large families typically opt for larger coolers, but sometimes multiple units of smaller dimensions fit the insides of vehicles better and are far less heavy and cumbersome to handle when they are filled with food and ice. Factors in determining cooler capacity include calculating the volume of food you'll need to keep cool during your trip. Larger groups will need more food, and a five-day trip will require more cooler capacity than a three-day trip. Then there's the volume of ice or re-freezable gel packs. You'll need to designate one-third to one-half of the cooler capacity for ice or other frozen goods to put the chill on your perishables.

Construction of the cooler plays a big part in its efficiency at keeping things cold. Most coolers have a hard-shelled outer plastic casing and a foam material

Coolers are sold in many sizes and configurations. Choose the one that best meets your camping needs, add ice, and keep your favorite foods and drinks cold.

between the outer shell and the plastic inner shell. Thicker walls and lids mean more insulation—and your food keeps cooler longer. Cheaper coolers generally have thinner walls than models on the pricier end. With any cooler, inspect the construction of the hinges, carrying handles, the drain plugs, and the latching mechanisms holding down the lid.

Some hybrid coolers are literally horizontal versions of a hotel minifridge. These car campers' gems plug into the 12-volt receptacles in your vehicle and keep your food chilled without ice. These are best left unplugged when you shut off your vehicle for the night, though, as they draw down your vehicle's battery to run the miniature compressor pump and other refrigeration components. These coolers are killer on long-distance trips, such as from coast to coast, or if you plan to camp while driving from the Lower 48 states to Alaska.

Styrofoam coolers spare you the elaborations above and offer a container made of pure insulation. Though they are far less durable than their plastic-shelled counterparts, these coolers are a fraction of the cost and will do the trick if you take precautions to avoid crushing or cracking their bottoms, sides, and lids. As kids we used to pretend they were thin-shelled dinosaur eggs, and they suited us well for years.

In the past decade, we've seen a proliferation of collapsible coolers. The outer shells are constructed of synthetic material, and the coolers integrate nylon loops for carrying handles and zippers for closing their lids. Wall thicknesses range from ½ to ¾ inch, and sizes range from personal lunchbox to big enough to cool food for a large group for about a day.

Some models offer plastic inserts to add rigidity. Though the inserts make these coolers less collapsible when they're empty, sandwiches and other food items retain their shape after rough rides in a boat or hours of jouncing down rough roads in a vehicle. They might not offer as much insulation as their hard plastic-coated counterparts, but you can cover them with sleeping bags and other camp materials in the car to increase their ability to hold in the cold.

TRASH

Depending upon where and how you plan to camp, expect a wide range of amenities when it comes to dealing with spent packaging, disposable garbage, and human waste. Many private campgrounds and some public campgrounds offer toilets, showers, and laundry facilities; others depend on large versions of an outhouse.

If your camping trip involves backpacking into remote wilderness areas, dealing with human waste jumps to another dimension: Leave No Trace (LNT) camping practices have been in place for decades in many states. Camping supply stores often have a backpacking section and offer several versions of fecal containment bags that rely on absorbent powders and other compounds to break down the organic matter so that the bags can be thrown into general trash containers upon reentering civilization. An increasing number of trailheads to remote areas now have specific containers for the human waste bags. An alternative method of disposing of human waste involves digging "cat holes" 6 to 8 inches deep in dark, organic soils and at least 200 feet from any open stream or lake. Cover feces with the same soil you dug out. In desert areas where the soil lacks high concentrations of organic matter, bury feces 4 inches deep so that the heat of the sun can accelerate decomposition. Backpacking sections of outdoors stores will often display lightweight plastic shovels for that purpose.

Recycling

Some states have embraced recycling of other solid waste more than others. Look for containers dedicated to glass, aluminum, and paper products. However, if you are a conscientious recycler at home and suspect that you won't find ample facilities at the campground, consider packing along extra trash bags or plastic mini totes to accommodate the various recyclables. Or you can mix them together in one bag and perform your solid waste separation when you return home.

A handy way to minimize camp waste is to remove packaging and recycle it at home before you head off into the hills (precycling). New headlamps, cookware, tents, and other camping equipment frequently arrive at stores with a combination of twisted wire, tape, and rubber bands or otherwise secured in elaborate plastic and cardboard packaging. Though most dehydrated food comes in foil-lined plastic pouches, many favorite high-protein snacks such as oysters, clams, shrimp, salmon, and other fish come in steel cans.

Don't expect the empties to melt and disappear in a campfire. Smash them flat with the blunt backside of a lightweight hatchet or with stones and pack them out. The same goes for aluminum. A common misconception is that aluminum cans melt in a campfire, but with a melting point of 1,221°F, chances are good that remnants of the cans will be left in the ashes.

A plastic bottle containing sports drinks or other electrolyte concoctions can double as a water bottle after you've consumed its colorful contents. Otherwise, remove the lids, twist bottles tightly into wrinkled, raisin-like shapes to drive out excess air (reducing bulk), and then screw the lids on tightly to create a vacuum and keep the bottles collapsed. As your trip progresses, think of ways to compress and consolidate your trash for the long trek back to the trailhead.

CHARLIE GOES CAMPING

While some define the wanigan as a temporary shelter, highly mobile on wheels or set up within a boat or raft, my understanding is that it contains only your kitchen goods and that you sleep in a tent or other arrangement nearby. I had one, and it proved pivotal in keeping all my camping utensils—and more—in their proper places.

To put this all in context, I was way into canoes when I turned 16. Sure, we all wanted our driver's licenses and a chance to drive the family car (alone!), but far higher on my short list of wants was a 17-foot aluminum canoe.

Having saved every penny from my summer jobs hauling hay bales and even babysitting, I purchased my dream canoe and launched it—only to discover that with my weight in the stern, the bow rose high out of the water. That meant about half the keel was in the water. The canoe tracked terribly when it was calm and became impossible to maneuver in more than a whisper of a breeze. I grew disenchanted that I had chosen a watercraft not designed for solo travel. Though I enjoyed the good company, extra paddling power, and extra weight of Chris, my other brother, Matt, or my sisters, Elizabeth and Annie, up front in the bow, I had envisioned the canoe as a vessel in which I could spend a lot of time alone on the water to sort out the stuff that comes in the aftermath of puberty. As luck would have it, my brother Chris had done a bit of reading about historical canoe travel and discovered the wanigan. (I should mention that he's always been an accomplished builder and finish carpenter, while I can hardly drive a straight nail.)

One day he up and builds a wanigan with dividers for dishes, pots, and pans, a complete kitchen 36 inches long, and a hinged door across its top. It fit snugly across the width of my canoe just behind the forward thwart. By then I'd acquired a large collection of cooking goods that included heavy cast-iron frying pans and most of the stuff mentioned in this chapter. I loaded the wanigan with my supplies, and there was even room for some food, a Hudson Bay ax, and a handsaw. But the best surprise awaited me when I loaded the wanigan into the canoe and discovered that it worked as a counterweight when I paddled from the stern. With my bow down and plenty of keel in the water, I was ready to start solo trip camping in my canoe.

Pack it in; pack it out.

All of it.

CAMP CHAIRS

Though camp chairs might seem to add extra bulk and complication to your packing, you'll spend a surprising amount of time in them at camp, even with a plethora of other activities filling your days. Without a table, you'll sit in the chairs with plates of food on your lap, and hang time around a campfire just isn't the same without taking a load off your legs, ankles, and feet.

Camp chairs have come down steadily in price through the years. At the same time, innovative designs have made them more collapsible. Many models incorporate arm rests with mesh drink holders, side pockets and other amenities. You'll want to purchase at least one chair for each member of your family or group, and maybe throw in a couple extras for the new friends you'll make at camp.

By day, campers explore the beach; come nightfall, the firepit and camp chairs become the epicenter of activity.

There's nothing like a sweet muffin to satisfy a hungry young camper.

CHAPTER 7

GRITS AND FIXIN'S
(LIFE BEYOND S'MORES)

NOWHERE DOES FOOD TASTE BETTER than when we're camping. It can be charred to a crisp or turn into a meal that would wind up in the trash can at home, but out here it's not only tasty but memorable.

Preparation is key. The more you can do at home to prearrange meals, the easier it is to churn out delicious offerings around the campfire. Certain entrees are best prepared in their entirety at home, while others can be staged by combining ingredients in an airtight storage container in the convenience of your kitchen then tossing them together as main dishes and cooking them up at camp.

Then again, some food just screams to be made from scratch in the great outdoors.

Much of what will go down in the realm of cooking when you get to camp will be predicated upon your heat source. It's all in the timing. Cooking outdoors with the rustic counterpart (fire) of the appliances you use at home will require your judgment whether meals are done or not. Knowing the intricacies of the heat sources described below will help you nail it when it comes to cooking times.

CAMPFIRE

The blaze that crackles and warms your backside from 5 feet away will be too hot for cooking entrees wrapped in foil packets and roasting hot dogs or marshmallows, and may threaten to singe your eyebrows when you come near. But it's a great start toward building a bed of coals that will cook your meals consistently

Campfire cooking takes more time than at home—and there might be a learning curve—but it's worth it. Experiment and enjoy.

and to perfection. If you intend to cook with a campfire, build it at least 45 minutes ahead of time. The trick is to pile on a sufficient armload of wood early on then leave it to burn down to glowing orange coals. A common mistake among campers not experienced in the art of cooking with fire is to feed it wood on a continuous basis. The resultant flames prove way too intense and char vegetables, meats, and other foods contained within packets, as well as threaten to catch grease on fire within flying pans, Dutch ovens, or other cooking vessels using oils or butter to keep food from sticking. The beauty of a deep bed of coals is that you can stir them, bringing warmer ones to the top to maintain continued heat. If this all sounds too exacting, do not dismay. Experiment. That's what camping's all about.

Grills

So maybe cooking over an open flame isn't your thing. That's fine. There are a number of portable grills on the market that you can take with you to cook up your favorite camp meals.

CHARCOAL GRILLS

These lightweight, inexpensive gems come in sizes not much larger than a basketball in diameter and run all the way to large models with legs that stand them waist high. In any event, choose a grill with a tight-fitting cover and vents in both its bottom and top. Adjusting the vents properly controls the heat and keeps fatty meats such as sausages, hot dogs, steaks, and other cuts of meat from catching fire yet cooks them perfectly in the center.

Like campfires, when it comes to cooking, charcoal grills need lead time to burn down to the right temperature. Fuel for these grills, charcoal briquettes, are purchased in large paper bags, poured into a small pile within the grill, then lit with a match to crumpled paper under a charcoal chimney or kindled with small sticks or paper within the pile. Charcoal lighting fluid is sold separately but often on shelves near the briquettes at most convenience

When coals turn orange, it's time to throw on the goodies.

stores. "Self-lighting" briquettes contain lighter fluid within. With either version, light a small pile of briquettes (about 3 pounds will cook a meal for the entire family) and let them burn with enough ventilation that they begin turning from black to white. You will notice that they turn white near their edges at first. When they are completely white, or the color of ash, it's time to throw on the goodies, cover them with a lid, and adjust the vents to allow the briquettes to burn evenly.

PROPANE GRILLS

Propane grills are among the most convenient; you turn on the gas supply, light them up, and they're ready to go within minutes. An added luxury with most propane models is that you can regulate the flame easily by adjusting the flow of gas to the burner. Just turn the knob (or knobs in some cases) up or down to regulate the heat. Many larger grills come with a temperature gauge on their lids that allows you to regulate the temperature within the grill like your oven at home.

Propane grills offer controlled temperatures and can accommodate large groups at the campsite. Some have wheels and racks, but you can find compact "tailgater" versions, which don't take up much space in your vehicle.

PREMADE BREADS, BISCUITS, ROLLS, AND CUPCAKES

Though the recipes in the pages ahead can be thrown together and baked or cooked in a makeshift oven out at camp, convenience often dictates that these camp favorites be made at home and put into storage containers for the days ahead.

DINNER ROLL DOUGH/FRY BREAD

This longtime favorite can be prepared at home, stored in containers, and served up as fresh-baked bread at camp. The trick is to prepare it and eat it the next day, but it's also good frozen and warmed up later. Though just about any bread dough recipe will work, the milk and sugar in this one produce a sweet bread that will be a hit for years to come. **MAKES** TWO DOZEN ROLLS

Fry bread has been a camp favorite for generations. Roll it in sugar for extra delight.

INGREDIENTS

5¾ to 6¾ cups flour
¼ cup sugar
2 teaspoons salt
2 packages active dry yeast
1 cup water
1 cup milk
½ cup butter
1 egg

DIRECTIONS

1. Combine 2 cups of the flour with the sugar, salt, and yeast. Whisk well.

2. Heat water, milk, and butter to 120°F. Add the warm liquid to the dry ingredients; add the egg and mix for about 3 minutes. Stir in the remaining flour and knead until dough comes away cleanly from sides of bowl.

3. On a floured board, knead the dough until smooth and elastic. Cover with plastic in a greased bowl and let rise until doubled.

4. Punch down and pull dough into roll-size portions; flatten. Brown on both sides in a frying pan.

Option: Toss the fresh-fried flatbread into a paper bag containing sugar. Shake. Remove. Enjoy.

ASH BISCUITS

These tasty treats become prescriptive when it's time to boost morale or when the camping family wants to experience a hint of survivalist cooking. The prep is simple: Visit a grocery store ahead of time and grab a couple cardboard tubes of frozen or refrigerated biscuit dough. Most of these have been packaged with the dough cut into handy biscuit portions already. For even more fun, pack them discreetly and keep them hidden from the other campers. At some point when you've built a fire, break out the biscuit dough, crack open the tubes against a stone, and hand out the biscuits. Campers can set the biscuits on hot rocks, skewer them onto sticks, or place them close to the embers. The idea is to bake them near a source of heat then brush off the ashes when they've turned golden brown. The smell of fresh-baked bread goes a long way toward effecting positive attitude. The biscuits are savory enough as is, but they enter another realm if you have also smuggled along a cube of butter.

Lemon cream cheese rolls might just be the best camp breakfast you'll ever have.

LEMON CREAM CHEESE ROLLS

These tasty breakfast rolls are created and baked at home and served cold in camp, or wrap them in aluminum foil to warm near the side of the campfire. For the dough, use the Dinner Roll/Fry Bread recipe described earlier in this chapter.

MAKES APPROXIMATELY 2 DOZEN ROLLS

DIRECTIONS

1. Preheat oven to 350°F.

2. Allow dough to rise in a large bowl with cloth cover; punch it back down.

3. Remove dough and roll out to form a rectangle on a flour-coated surface.

4. Now, here's where the flavoring fun begins. Spread the cream cheese over the rolled-out dough. Top with the lemon fruit filling. Sprinkle zest evenly throughout the mix.

5. Roll out dough, starting at the long edge. Pinch ends shut.

6. Cut rolls into approximately 1½-inch slices. Line two 13 × 9-inch cookie sheets with parchment paper. Place rolls slightly apart. Let rise until double.

7. Bake for 25 to 30 minutes until golden brown.

8. Mix ingredients of glaze together to desired consistency. Drizzle glaze on the rolls while they're still warm.

INGREDIENTS

Dinner Roll/Fry Bread Dough (page 87)

1 (8-ounce) package cream cheese

1 (9.5-ounce) jar lemon fruit filling

½ teaspoon grated lemon zest

FOR THE GLAZE:

1 cup powdered sugar

1 tablespoon milk

½ teaspoon lemon juice

Cheesecake minis with whipped cream and sliced fresh strawberries

CHEESECAKE MINIS

Dazzle your camping friends and blow them off their lawn chairs when you break out the Cheesecake Minis. This delectable camping dessert ranks high in terms of creativity—and presentation. But the minis are easy to make. The secret lies in purchasing premade mini graham cracker crusts at the grocery store. For toppings try blueberries or thinly sliced strawberries, bananas, peaches—any fruit of your liking. **MAKES** APPROXIMATELY 1 DOZEN MINI CHEESECAKES

INGREDIENTS

2 (8-ounce) packages cream cheese

3 eggs

⅔ cup sugar

½ teaspoon almond extract

1 dozen individual cheesecake crusts

1 cup thinly sliced strawberries

1 can whipped cream

DIRECTIONS

1. Preheat oven to 350°F.

2. Beat cream cheese, eggs, sugar, and almond extract together until smooth and thick. Fill the cheesecake crusts.

3. Place the small foil cups on a cookie sheet lined with parchment paper. Bake in the preheated oven for 25 to 30 minutes.

4. Let cool to room temperature. Keep refrigerated until ready to serve.

5. Remove from refrigerator. Arrange in airtight storage container.

6. When you're ready to serve at camp, garnish with strawberries and whipped cream.

CHERRY-FILLED CHOCOLATE CUPCAKES

Dark chocolate lovers don't need to compromise their cravings at camp.

MAKES APPROXIMATELY 1½ DOZEN CUPCAKES

DIRECTIONS

1. Preheat oven to 350°F.

2. Mix flour, baking soda, baking powder, cocoa, and dash of salt.

3. In another bowl, cream the sugar and coconut oil; add eggs and vanilla. Add the flour mixture to the wet mixture alternately with milk. Don't overmix.

4. Arrange parchment paper cupcake liners inside muffin pan (1 dozen). Fill each cupcake liner ⅓ full (approximately ⅓ cup) with the batter. Spoon in 1 tablespoon cherry filling. Cover with another ⅓ cup cupcake batter.

5. Bake 15 to 17 minutes in preheated oven. Let cool.

6. Frost and store in airtight containers.

FROSTING

1. Mix together the confectioners' sugar and dark cocoa powder.

2. Cream in softened coconut oil. Add vanilla and blend in milk, 1 tablespoon at a time, until desired consistency.

INGREDIENTS

1⅓ cups flour
¼ teaspoon baking soda
2 teaspoons baking powder
¾ cup dark cocoa
1 dash salt
1½ cups sugar
3 tablespoons coconut oil, softened
2 eggs
1 teaspoon vanilla
1 cup milk
1 (9.5-ounce) jar cherry fruit filling

Creamy Dark Chocolate Frosting

4 cups confectioners' sugar
¾ cup dark cocoa powder
1 cup coconut oil, softened
2 teaspoons vanilla
5 tablespoons milk

Cherry-filled chocolate cupcakes

Granola makes a
great breakfast
and also a great
trail snack.

CHERYL'S ULTRA GRANOLA

For years, Cheryl churned out granola in multiple flavors as a commercial venture after campers, bikers, hikers, trail runners, and folks engaging in literally every outdoor adventure created demand that had her hovering over industrial-size mixers and working long nights in a bakery. These days she makes granola on a much smaller scale at home. We eat it almost every day for breakfast (I like mine with yogurt) and prefer it to trail mix on our many outings. **MAKES** 16 CUPS

DIRECTIONS

1. Preheat oven to 325°F.

2. Mix together dry ingredients (through salt).

3. In a separate bowl, mix together the honey, maple syrup, and coconut oil.

4. Combine the wet and dry ingredients. Add the sliced almonds or substitutes.

5. Line a cookie sheet with parchment paper. Divide the mixture and spread evenly on two 13 × 9-inch cookie sheets.

6. Bake for approximately 25 minutes, or until golden brown. Remove from oven and let cool completely.

7. Break up granola to desired consistency and place in a large bowl. Add dried cranberries or other fruits. Store granola in airtight containers or ziplock bags.

INGREDIENTS

8 cups rolled oats
2 cups shredded coconut
1 tablespoon cinnamon
1 teaspoon ginger
½ teaspoon nutmeg
1 teaspoon salt
½ cup honey
½ cup maple syrup
½ cup coconut oil, softened
2 cups sliced almonds
(optional: sunflower seeds, cashews, other nuts)
1 cup dried cranberries
or fruit of your choice

MEAT-N-GREET

In this simple finger food, meat meets cheese in a combo sure to please. Midafternoon snacks are a must after a brisk hike or a chilly swim, and setting these handy high-protein snacks out on the table will take the edge off hunger without ruining appetites for dinner.

INGREDIENTS

1 package cheese of your choice (cheddar, jalapeño, Swiss)

1 package sliced deli meat of your choice (turkey, ham, pastrami)

DIRECTIONS

1. Cut your favorite chunk of cheese into approximately ½-inch cubes.

2. Cut the deli meat lengthwise to form long strips in which to roll the cheese.

3. Roll up the cheese inside the meat; insert a toothpick to hold the combo together.

Meat-N-Greet is perfect for a quick afternoon protein pick-me-up.

CAMPFIRE FOIL WRAPS

You might have heard them called shore dinners, campfire packets, food packs, hobo dinners, meal-in-ones, or other monikers, but the following recipe for Campfire Foil Wraps just might be the end-all to your best outdoor meal ever. For practicality, it helps to assemble the meals ahead of time and pack them into your cooler so that you can toss them onto a campfire grill or cook them over briquettes or on a gas grill.

As a variation, try cubed chicken breast, green peppers, frozen corn, mandarin orange slices, spinach leaves, and your favorite spices.

The creativity begins in your home kitchen and culminates at a campfire in your camp.

Note: The ingredients, accompanying spices, and condiments in this recipe will vary according to personal taste. **MAKES** 1 WRAP EACH

INGREDIENTS

Meat (sausage, pork, beef, various types of fish, chicken)

Vegetables (green, red, yellow peppers, onions, shallots, celery, broccoli, cauliflower, carrots, corn—you name it)

Precooked rice or sliced/ cubed raw potatoes

Salt and pepper to taste (optional: grilling spices)

Butter

DIRECTIONS

1. Lay a generous rectangle (12 × 18 inches) of heavy-duty aluminum foil out across a kitchen counter or table. Roll out parchment paper on top of the foil.

2. Begin assembling the meal. Start with the meats, as they require hotter temperature to cook in sync with vegetables that only need to be steamed. **Option:** For a fun variation, start with a large leaf of collard greens at the very bottom of the meal to kick in extra flavors and help prevent scorching.

3. Add your favorite vegetables. Slice, dice, or chop vegetables into bite-size chunks and arrange them in a pile on top of the meats in the center of the parchment paper.

4. Add precooked rice or raw potato slices. Season to taste. (*Note:* Be careful not to overfill each pack: more than 3 cups is too much.)

5. Add a thick pat or two of butter, which will melt down and give rich flavor to the other ingredients within the packet.

6. Roll up all the ingredients tightly inside the parchment paper; give the excess paper a few twists or folds to help it stay shut. Roll up the aluminum foil to encase the whole mix. Twist and fold the ends of the foil so that precious juices won't leak out.

7. Roll the first packet inside a second layer of foil. If you've done it right, the packet won't feel floppy or loose.

8. Place the packets on the grill. You'll know the wraps are done when the scents of the ingredients begin wafting your way. No matter how tightly you've sealed the pouches, the flavorful juices will boil and steam will escape. You won't be able to stave off your hunger any longer. It's time to eat.

DUTCH OVEN MEALS

When foil packets aren't enough to feed a large group of campers, it's time to break out the cast-iron Dutch oven. To some outdoor chefs, these heavy kettles are the last piece of cookware you'll ever need. For more than a century America's backwoods dwellers have used them for frying meat, rendering fats, simmering soups, and baking rolls, cakes, bread loaves, and cornbread. The beauty of a Dutch oven is that it's also a deep version of a frying pan and can be used for making fry bread or to brown meat that later becomes the stock of stew, to be cooked in the selfsame kettle. Fill them with a sufficient level of cooking oil and they become deep fryers for homemade doughnuts, french fries, fish, or chicken. But there's more: Grease up the Dutch oven, place bread dough in the bottom, put on the lid, bury it in coals, and retrieve it a short while later to enjoy beautiful browned bread.

The trick to achieving perfectly baked breads, cakes, and desserts in Dutch ovens without burning the bottoms is to double the amount of red-hot coals or charcoal briquettes placed on the top of the oven. For an estimated oven temperature of 350°F with a 10-inch model, try 7 briquettes (or an equivalent in wood coals) under the bottom with 14 on top. Larger ovens require more: A Dutch oven with a 14-inch bottom would require 11 coals on the bottom and 22 on the top.

Most Dutch ovens include a heavy wire handle that allows them to be hung over fires or extracted from a hot bed of coals. Camping supply stores sell accessory tools for hanging the pots above an open fire or handling them when they're hot. A pair of heavy leather work gloves (welding gloves are incredible) provide both comfort and safety when cooking with Dutch ovens.

Where Dutch ovens differ among manufacturers is in the style of their lids. Though all lids fit snugly on top of the lower units, some lids are dome-shaped; others are flat with a rim around the outside to accommodate a heaping pile of coals on their tops. The latter style lends itself better to holding hot coals on top, while coals tend to fall off the dome-shaped lids. The flat tops are our favorite—the ability to stack more hot coals on top ensures even heat from above and prevents burning breads and other baked goods on bottom. If you can't find a flat-topped model, fear not. One trick with dome-shaped lids is to heap a tall pile of coals all around the oven to support a layer of coals on top. If that's too much heat for what's cooking inside, heap ashes or spent coals along the sides to support the hot coals on top. Depending on what you're cooking, another option would be to invert the lid so that it forms a dish in which to place the coals. This method cuts down on height within the oven, and you'll have to adjust the quantity of recipes so that the handle of the inverted lid doesn't protrude into your cornbread.

A savory recipe for campers in any weather, Dutch oven chicken stew sticks to the ribs and will remain a camp favorite for years to come.

DUTCH OVEN CHICKEN STEW

A couple of nights before you go camping, roast a whole chicken (seasoned with salt, pepper, and poultry seasoning) in your oven at home. Add sufficient water to keep the meat moist. Let it cool overnight. The next day, remove the chicken, place it on a cutting board, and cut the meat into bite-size cubes. Save the gelatinous substance at the bottom of the pot; it will turn into a savory broth later on in the process. **MAKES** 8–10 SERVINGS

DIRECTIONS

1. Set aside the meat and gel in a storage container.

2. In a small pan, cook the rice; cool and store in a container. Next, chop or slice the onion, celery, red peppers, carrots, kale or spinach, mushrooms, and Italian parsley.

3. Place each ingredient in a separate storage container, and stack the containers in your cooler.

4. At camp and with a campfire burning, place the half cube of butter into the Dutch oven. When the butter melts, add the onion, celery, peppers, mushrooms, and carrots.

5. Sauté the medley to your liking; add chicken and the chicken gel. Add enough water to submerge all ingredients and then the cooked rice. Bring to a boil. Add kale or spinach to the boiling mixture minutes before serving. Top the dish with Italian parsley and season to taste.

INGREDIENTS

1 chicken, roasted and cut into bite-size cubes, preserving gel

2 cups cooked rice

1 onion, chopped

1 bunch celery, chopped

2 red peppers, chopped

6 carrots, sliced

2 bunches kale or spinach

2 cups sliced mushrooms

½ cup Italian parsley

½ cube butter

Water

Dutch oven baked oatmeal is ready to eat.

DUTCH OVEN BAKED OATMEAL

We've all had oatmeal in our youth for energy and in our later years for its merits of lowering cholesterol and adding fiber. But in camp, this recipe takes taste to the next dimension while providing energy to meet our morning demands. This recipe is for an 8-quart Dutch oven. **MAKES** 8–10 SERVINGS

INGREDIENTS

½ cup melted butter, plus more for greasing Dutch oven

½ cup coconut oil, melted

1 cup maple syrup

½ cup brown sugar

1 teaspoon vanilla

1 teaspoon salt

4 eggs

1 tablespoon baking powder

3 cups rolled oats

2¾ cup quick oats

¼ teaspoon cinnamon

¼ teaspoon nutmeg

2 cups milk, or your choice of almond, coconut or other milks

1 cup nuts or dried fruit (optional)

DIRECTIONS

1. Mix together melted butter, melted coconut oil, maple syrup, brown sugar, vanilla, and salt. Mix in eggs. Stir in baking powder, oats, cinnamon, and nutmeg. Add milk and optional fruit or nuts; mix.

2. Store these mixed ingredients in a plastic container in your cooler until you're ready to cook.

3. When it's time to bake: Liberally butter the Dutch oven on its bottom and sides. Add the oatmeal and pack slightly to form a smooth layer.

4. Set the oven on a grill positioned at least 6 inches above a bed of coals which are red hot but not putting out flames. The idea is to apply low heat to the bottom of the cast-iron Dutch oven so that the oatmeal doesn't burn. You're shooting for a cooking time of 20 to 25 minutes. If the lid of your Dutch oven is flat, sprinkle just a few briquettes or glowing wood coals on top for oven-like heat.

5. Check frequently. Serve this savory dish with a bit of heavy cream or milk.

DUTCH OVEN PINEAPPLE UPSIDE-DOWN CAKE

Try this for an evening treat at your campsite. Much of cooking in the wild involves experimentation. **MAKES** 8–10 SERVINGS

DIRECTIONS

1. Melt the butter in the bottom of the Dutch oven. Spread brown sugar evenly across the melted butter.

2. Place pineapple slices atop the brown sugar and then a Maraschino cherry in the center of each slice. Save the pineapple and Maraschino cherry juices and add to the cake mix as a substitute for the water specified in the recipe.

3. Add the eggs and oil (if required by mix) and pineapple and cherry juices (add water if required to bring the mix to proper consistency) to the cake mix per the recipe on the box. Pour cake mix over the brown sugar and pineapple.

4. Bake approximately 20 minutes or until cake is browned and a knife comes out clean.

INGREDIENTS

⅓ cup butter

½ cup brown sugar

1 small can sliced pineapple

Maraschino cherries (for placing in the centers of pineapples)

1 box yellow cake mix

Eggs, if cake mix requires

Oil, if cake mix requires

Poached eggs camped among a medley of fruit on the plate are ready for a hungry camper.

MOCK POACHED EGGS

This breakfast campfire special requires very little prep at home, as it relies on the time-tested hack of storing eggs in a reusable bottle. The trick is to crack the eggs into a bottle with a 1½-inch cap, which enables you to pour them back out, one egg at a time. Some folks suggest breaking the yolks or pre-scrambling the eggs, but even after rugged trips, we've been able to retrieve the eggs with the yolks intact. This egg transporting trick is a recycler's dream, and you can fit a dozen eggs or more into most bottles. **MAKES** ONE MOCK POACHED EGG PER CUP IN MUFFIN TINS (6 OR 12)

INGREDIENTS

6 or 12 eggs
Salt and pepper or other seasonings to taste

DIRECTIONS

1. Line an aluminum muffin tin with parchment paper baking cups. Pour one egg in each cup. Add salt and pepper, or season to taste.

2. Place the tin on a makeshift rack above campfire coals and cover with aluminum foil to hold in the heat.

3. Cooking times vary according to intensity of the fire, so check the eggs often. Pull them away from the fire when they're done to your liking. Serve with fresh fruit or other breakfast foods.

GRILLED CAMP SANDWICHES

Though you can wrap your sandwiches in aluminum foil and toss them on the coals of a campfire, gas-fired grill, or charcoal briquets, we have come to love a contraption known as a broiler grilling basket. These campfire gadgets are commonly sold at camping or outdoor cooking supply stores. They are fairly inexpensive, and about their only limit is your creativity. They've proven themselves extremely versatile when it comes to building s'mores and grilling multiple sandwiches, fish, steaks, or other cuts of meat.

The broiler grilling basket comes into its own when making batches of sandwiches for a hungry crew. The grilled sandwiches require no more than packing ingredients into separate storage containers and tossing them into your camp cooler before you leave home. At camp, fire up the grill, light up a batch of briquettes, or let the campfire dwindle down to white/orange coals. Break out the bread and other ingredients and assemble cold deli sandwiches with layers of meat, vegetables, cheese slices, and condiments like you would at home. The

When the cheese is melted and the bread is toasted, your sandwich is done.

beauty of making sandwiches in the here and now is that the condiments and other wet ingredients won't turn the bread soggy if you don't get to making the sandwiches right away. **MAKES** 1 SANDWICH

INGREDIENTS

Presliced deli meats
Presliced deli cheeses
Leafy vegetables
Condiments of choice

DIRECTIONS

1. Assemble the sandwiches according to each camper's likes.

2. Arrange sandwiches neatly within the open grilling broiler basket. Close the basket and slide the locking ring down the handle to keep the two halves from opening.

3. Toast sandwiches on one side then flip the basket to toast the other side. The grilled sandwiches are done when the cheese begins oozing out from the bread. That's a sure sign they're perfect.

HOMEMADE MARSHMALLOW CUBES

Though you can buy marshmallows by the bushel in the store, there are many online recipes that will guide you through the process of making marshmallows that will not only produce cube-shaped renditions after you cut them from a solid cake but also earn rave reviews when you discover their unique flavors.

The recipes vary, but generally they're a combination of granulated sugar, corn syrup, cold water, gelatin, vanilla extract, and confectioners' sugar, which keeps them from sticking together. Turning out a successful batch relies on paying attention to each recipe's detail and a good electric mixer.

These marshmallows roast quicker over a campfire than their store-bought counterparts. Watch them carefully, and pull them away from the fire immediately after they begin to droop from your stick. The consistency and flavor of these homespun marshmallows enter another dimension when used in s'mores.

OVER THE FIRE AND ON THE FLY

This do-it-yourselfer method of making meals might prove the most fun of all. But first a couple requirements:

1. The camping area in which you're staying will allow you to cut and sharpen sticks or small branches to form marshmallow and hot dog sticks. (Bamboo shish kabob skewers can be used as a substitute if necessary.)

2. You can fire up a grill or build a campfire.

The setup for these meals demands not much more than ripping open a package of sausages, hot dogs, or precooked shrimp, skewering them onto a stick,

Kids with sticks, meat, and fire naturally make a meal on their own.

S'mores are great but gooey, flavorful, and fun for an evening around the fire.

and holding them over hot coals. Depending on the ages and dexterity of your camping family members—and an ever-present mind for safety—parents may want to push the hot dog onto the sharpened stick. But it's fun to hand the kids a stick, point them to the hot dogs, and let them try it for themselves.

An interesting development among family members around a fire is what constitutes "done." Invariably, some kids will put the meat into the open flames, charring its outsides in a matter of seconds; others will turn the meat methodically, mimicking a rotisserie.

The same goes for that perennial favorite over-the-fire dessert: roasted marshmallows. Some campers twirl them slowly over the heat until they turn a rich caramel brown; others center them directly in the hottest of flames, let them catch fire, retract them from the inferno, and blow them out like a large candle. It's all a matter of personal preference, and it's fun to watch large groups and the variability in what constitutes a properly roasted marshmallow.

INSTANT EVERYTHING

From instant oatmeal and instant gourmet coffee in the morning to dense snack bars, fruit leather, and carbohydrate gels in the afternoon to freeze-dried entrees and desserts at night, camping supply companies have thought of it all. Just add hot water. While dining on straight dehydrated food can get old after a week, the lightweight meals offer an appreciable range of eats on backpacking trips or other situations where weight and bulk become an issue.

Entrees range from sweet-and-sour pork to beef Stroganoff to spaghetti and meatballs—and much more. Desserts include peach cobbler and other instant delectables, while scrambled eggs and bacon are common choices for breakfast. Though dehydrated potato slices have been available in bulk since the 1980s, instant food companies have refined choices to hash browns that soak in warm water for less than 15 minutes then reconstitute to a texture you would expect to find at a restaurant. Most of the meals are prepared by pouring hot water into the thick foil envelopes, stirring the contents with a long spoon or smooth stick, and resealing the pouches so that the rice, chunks of meat, dried vegetables, and other ingredients reconstitute into some semblance of what they were before they hit high-temperature dehydrators.

An important first step in preparing freeze-dried meals, however, is to fish out any silica gel packets that have been added to the pouches to absorb moisture.

Some campers purchase a quality dehydrator and enjoy drying their favorite fruits, vegetables, meats (they make great jerky out of steak strips), spices, and other ingredients and making their own meals to go.

HYDRATION

Lemonade. At one end of the spectrum, it's a pitcher full of fresh-squeezed lemon juice, dozens of ice cubes, and copious amounts of sugar. At the other end it's a pinch of powdered crystals added to water in a paper cup. Either way, you'll need liquids—and plenty of them—as camping kicks the metabolism and the body needs water to convert food into energy to move and stay warm. Proper hydration throughout the day comes to some campers naturally, while others charge ahead in the sun for hours without a thought of taking a drink, only to realize they are severely dehydrated. Dizziness upon standing is one sure sign of dehydration, as is the lack of elasticity in the skin between your knuckles and wrist on the back of your hand.

The easiest way to create a higher hydrating consciousness among campers in the latter category is to place water containers in conspicuous spots, such as on picnic tables, near stumps, on benches or on stools in the shade of trees. Leakproof containers should be filled after breakfast in the morning and stuffed into daypacks or the cupholders in the family vehicle.

Slices of watermelon, honeydew, or cantaloupe provide a sneaky way to keep kids and finicky adults hydrated throughout the day. Orange, lemon, or lime slices (sometimes all three) added to water help encourage drinking more.

You'll want to cover pitchers with suitable lids to keep the water free of insects and reduce evaporation. Melon slices are best stored in sealed containers, as their sweetness attracts ants, wasps, and other unwanted intruders.

In hot weather or where strenuous activity demands an intake of more than a quart of water per hour, electrolytes need to be added to help the body retain water within its cells. Flooding the body with pure water can trigger the onset of hyponatremia, which is basically the depletion of sodium. Severe cases produce such symptoms as nausea, vomiting, and headache, but often muscle cramps in

CHARLIE GOES CAMPING

Not that I have anything against dehydrated camping meals—in fact I have my faves—but imagine a night when Cheryl and I and our good friend Ty headed out camping in winter. We'd traveled all day on snowshoes and arrived at camp with our clothes wet from perspiration. We realized we needed a huge injection of calories to be able to sleep warmly through the night. To cut down on weight, we hadn't packed a tent and planned to sleep on the snow, under the stars. Though we had doubled up on portions of dehydrated entrees when we had thrown together our food the night before, we realized it would not be enough. Our reserve? Several packets of instant oatmeal and instant coffee that we'd intended to eat the next morning. At the side of a roaring campfire, we melted snow, brought the water to a boil in our small aluminum pot, and poured it into the pouches of freeze-dried sweet and sour pork.

While we recounted our experiences of camping in one of Alaska's most remote areas around the glow of the fire, we suddenly detected a scent that mimicked a large steakhouse wafting our way. We had noticed Ty tossing a large blob of something wrapped in aluminum foil into the fire just minutes before. We inquired about its contents. He took a slender willow stick, flipped the packet over, and divulged that it contained a massive rib-eye steak. Turned out, he had fired up his grill at home the night before, tossed on an extra steak, and then wrapped it in several layers of foil.

the legs show up first. The cure is to keep salt tablets on hand, or mix water with powdered electrolyte. There are myriad electrolyte supplements to choose from, available in many grocery stores or shops catering to marathon runners.

Though some punch mixes and carbonated beverages hit the spot on a hot day, they're more about flavor and less about value in terms of proper hydration.

Watermelon can be a great way to keep kids hydrated.

Moments later, we heard the fat sizzling inside the foil. The steak thawed, expelling its juices. The foil expanded, and the scent of grilling spices made their escape. Our mouths watered at the thought of a juicy chunk of meat.

Ty, like all our camping friends, is generous to a fault. He shared the huge steak, and we countered with paltry portions of our rice and pork. We slept soundly and woke at first light to freshly falling snow. We had our oatmeal and coffee and began the long, ethereal trip home.

I recently got to pay Ty's trick forward when I led a crew on a backpacking trip with tools to improve trails in one of Alaska's state parks. The trail into the work area was steep, so weight was a factor. We'd packed dehydrated entrees, a minimal assortment of fruit and vegetables for the vegetarians in the group, and a variety of trail mixes. Before we'd left town I'd stuffed a large tube of summer sausage, two large packages of presliced salami, six large bagels, and two packets of cream cheese into my pack. It always amazes me how morale picks up a couple notches when you surprise a group with somewhat frivolous food items. It gave me great satisfaction to watch happy campers roasting chunks of the sausage over the open fire on sticks and then combine cheese and salami on top of bagels with cream cheese to create a tasty sandwich. As for me, I lightened my pack by nearly 4 pounds in one night.

A family loses
track of time
building rock
cairns on a beach.

PLAY

Maybe it was day four, but I can't be sure, as we'd lost track of time on one of the remotest beaches in Alaska's extreme southwest. We had come to the abandoned village of Ikatan on Unimak Island to show our daughter, Lindsey, and son, Clarence, where we'd lived out entire summers so long ago. We'd left when they were too young to remember it. The years rolled on. They had advanced through middle school and were on the cusp of taking on summer jobs and other obligations that would prevent the four of us from again spending quality time together in a tent. It was Cheryl's idea to take this last family camping trip. But middle schoolers get bored quickly. They were done with hiking; sick of beachcombing, fishing, and gathering firewood.

So we salvaged empty 5-gallon buckets from the beach, filled them with fine gravel, moved the tent to the side, and filled in the holes and smoothed over spots that had made our beds uncomfortable. After we had improved the tent pad to our satisfaction, we reinforced driftwood poles that supported the insulators and wires to a powerful solar-powered electric fence that we'd packed to keep large brown bears out of our camp at night. On the fifth day we built a long bench from logs.

Lindsey thrilled us one afternoon with sandcastles and moats. We dug a deep hole in the cool gravel on the shady side of the tent, cleaned out a salvaged bucket with a lid, and buried it to serve as a refrigerator for our mayonnaise and butter. After the tide had fallen, we gathered small mollusks called chitons from under the cobbles, built a fire on the beach, and boiled them up. We also collected several long strands of ribbon kelp, laid them upon the hot rocks near the campfire, and roasted them until they tasted much like the seaweed used in sushi. Clarence gathered up some sand fleas, put them in a pouch of aluminum foil with a little butter, and cooked them up. They tasted somewhat like shrimp. Sure, we had plenty of other food, but the new activities energized us and put a creative spin on the day.

Girls run in sand on a hot summer day at camp.

CHAPTER 8

OUTDOOR GAMES

PLAY TAKES ON as many forms as campers care to create, and more often than not, the activity falls to the ownership of the group. Think of it as an inside joke. Funny. Intimate. Play can be a circle game to kill time under a tarp until a rain squall passes. It can be an impromptu arm-wrestling match at a picnic table while dinner simmers on a camp stove, or making improvements to the camp like we did out on Unimak Island that summer.

Props that can add fun activities to your campout, include playing cards, index cards and pencils, small lengths of twine or rope, nails, party hats, or an assortment of colored scarves.

NATURE ENTERTAINS

If you've forgotten the above-mentioned props, fear not; nature never shorts the creative camper when it comes to providing infinite forms of entertainment. One of our favorite pastimes as kids was to roam the woods with our pocketknives, cut stout branches and slender sticks, and attempt to build bows and arrows.

Birds, whales, and other sights on the water never get old when you're camping.

Other simple forms of entertainment include shoreside batting practice with a stout chunk of driftwood and the infinite supply of rocks. As kids we used to bat rocks out over the water until our arms ached. Taking a sharp stick to wet sand has been a favorite entertainment through the years. Write. Sculpt. Imagine.

If you're camping near water, another family activity to try is beachcombing, scavenging, or other creative ways to acquire the ingredients to build miniature sailboats. Boatbuilding can provide hours of entertainment and give everyone in camp a chance to express his or her unique approach to creating a similar object. Even more fun comes when the boats hit the water. Some sail along swiftly, while others dawdle in the waves. The opportunity for team building, empathy, and other life skills comes about when boats sink or don't move as their builders intended.

CHARLIE GOES CAMPING

Some years ago I had the privilege of training in a curriculum that outlined seven components to outdoor wilderness survival. Here in Alaska, disproportionate numbers of people perish from situations that involve plane crashes, mechanical problems with snowmobiles in remote travel, drowning, avalanches, falling down steep mountains, and myriad other circumstances that can turn an everyday outing into an all-out quest to survive. In more optimistic scenarios, mishaps turn into a long waiting game until folks discover you're missing and set out on a search. To my surprise, one of the seven survival components is play—as defined by the curriculum, any activity in which energy is expended to bring about the feeling of hope. Through the years, though, I've learned that you don't need to be in a survival situation before introducing play into the camping scheme to keep up morale.

Another variation is to create musical instruments with what nature provides and put on a family concert. Rocks and sticks smacked together and sand shaken in a paper bag make a perfect percussion section, and if that's not enough, incorporate pots, pans, or other cooking utensils to broaden the sound of your band. Hollow sticks or the dead stalks of local plants form the basis of a flutelike instrument, and a blade of grass stretched tightly between the base of the thumb and the fingertips mimics one of the woodwind instruments with just the right amount of exhaled breath.

Play in the camp setting often provides the perfect environment for building self-esteem, leadership, and problem-solving skills. A favorite outdoor activity with groups is to have them collect stones of different colors, sticks, branches, grasses, and other natural items and erect a monument that represents them as a group. For some, it becomes their first experience in consensus building and collaboration. For others, it challenges them to trust. This activity nearly always enhances communication skills for every member of the group.

If you're camping near the ocean, the outgoing tide will often expose hundreds, if not thousands, of clamshells. Take the kids to the beach. They'll spend hours constructing castles, miniature forts, and defined paths—even labyrinths—between each of their kingdoms with the seashells. Even more enlightening, many of the youngsters will create stories with imaginary characters who live in their kingdoms.

Treasure hunts rise to the top of the list in terms of high energy, laughter, and communication skills. As for the structure, it's basically a game of hide-and-seek. But instead of the leader counting to 100 while others hide in the woods, the goal is to listen to directions and then run and find and then return with an object the leader describes. Treasure hunts can be set up as an all-out race to run and fetch a specific object ("Bring me a pine cone.") or can incorporate mystery ("I'm thinking of something green, smaller than your hand, and it lives by the creek.").

A more elaborate version involves hiding treasures in the woods ahead of time, teaching basic compass skills and how to judge distance by pacing, then supplying contestants with hand-drawn maps that include compass bearings in degrees and distances to the treasures. With multiple groups, the energy level rises as competing groups chase one another. More often than not, the group in the lead makes panicked decisions, loses the course, and the challenge resumes as the groups reconsider their strategy and study the map.

Geocaching and other public orienteering venues post locations of caches (mostly waterproof tubes with a lid and a notebook and pencil within) online with an *X* on the map and latitude and longitude coordinates. It's great family fun to try and find them without using a Global Positioning System (GPS) device. Start with a map and compass, and take turns leading the way. The notebooks inside the protective tube or box at the sites often provide the names of previous visitors and their accounts of the weather, wildlife sightings, their quest to find the cache, and other information. Some caches might contain emergency supplies such as ultralight space blankets; others include disposable cameras for group pictures that eventually show up on community or club-based hiking websites or other social media.

BIRDS, BUGS, AND OTHER IDENTIFICATION

Bird-, bug-, and animal-watching falls in line with play. Pack along a pocket guide for bird identification, sit quietly as individuals or as a group, and guess how many species you think you can spot. Some camping areas offer interpretive programs and guided tours providing detailed information about the local flora and fauna. If yours doesn't, you as a family can embark on nature sorties of your own. Magnifying glasses, binoculars, spotting scopes, and various identification guides become the family entertainment centers of the outdoors as you discover a world extensively different from the one you left at home.

Though biodiversity theory suggests that the number of plant, fish, and animal species increases as you move toward latitudes near the equator and decreases as you move toward the poles, most states where you'll camp will have more than 400 species of birds. Some are migrants, passing through at various times of the year; others are residents and nest locally each summer. Families can keep a running list of the birds and animals sighted, and may spend hours watching them forage and care for their young.

Trees and plants are another great source of entertainment. They actually form communities where they complement one another in terms of capturing water, providing shade, and other qualities to sustain themselves and the wildlife that depends on them.

Or learn to track animals. Raccoons, skunks, rabbits, porcupines, possums, armadillos, deer, and bears all leave distinctly different tracks—and each animal makes different tracks when it's traveling, feeding, or fleeing. If weight is not an issue in packing for that next trip—and that next trip holds promise of sand along the banks of a river or a lake—include a few small bags of plaster of paris. Many interpretive programs with state and national parks and other nature centers offer animal tracking guides with supplemental information about the species that made them as well as the surrounding ecology. It's equally fun to acquire the knowledge as a

A red poll perches on a dead cattail near a lake in the Midwest. Binoculars become the new screen time when youths embrace the outdoor world around them.

Porcupines are approachable and fun to watch. Despite popular belief, they don't shoot their quills.

family, and in many cases the animal tracking and ecological studies meld perfectly with a homeschool curriculum. Now the fun part: the plaster. Find a well-defined set of animal tracks. Mix up the plaster, pour it into a single track, and let it harden. Brush away the loose sand or mud, and take home a lasting memory.

For other interpretive forms of play, check out the possibility of harvesting edible plants in your camping area. Many land management and other governmental agencies supply fact sheets, brochures, even books, and you'll find a wealth of online nutritional information to guide you toward the fun of making a wild salad in camp. Families wanting to combine fun with a sense of community service can link up with various conservation groups, put on their gloves, and help eradicate invasive species.

SKILLS

A guidebook on knots and a few lengths of colorful paracord or mountain climbing accessory cordage make for great play around camp. I like to teach groups how to tie some of the basic knots then organize knot-tying races around the campfire at night. In time, folks who like keeping their hands busy gravitate from the simple, utilitarian knots to those that have been created for decoration. Through the years it has been fun to watch youth as they gain proficiency in knowing when to use a particular knot to accommodate a particular task. Among all age-groups, knowledge of knots provides an avenue for mastery and pays huge dividends when it's time to lash poles together for the framework

CHARLIE GOES CAMPING

At the advent of our second summer camping together as a tight-knit family, my mother, ever the seamstress, created small white canvas bags with a strap long enough that we could throw them over a shoulder, like a purse. These "gadget bags," as she called them, had been designed with a buckle-down flap and had our names embroidered across the canvas with bright red thread. Inside the bags, she'd outfitted each of us with a powerful magnifying glass, tweezers, and pocket guides for bird and rock identification. We'd return from our forays to the lakeshore or deep in the woods each day with the little bags laden with treasures to share and take home as keepsakes. These days there's a mind-set to leave articles of nature untouched (it's the law in national and many state parks), but it never hurts to look. So the gadget bags can still rule with pocket identification guides, a magnifying glass, and possibly a pair of inexpensive, entry-level binoculars.

of a makeshift shelter or secure a tarp among trees in a storm.

An all-time favorite activity with groups of all ages has been to tie survival/friendship bracelets. Some bracelet designs depend on plastic snaps or buckles to secure them around the wrist, but many patterns require nothing more than finishing off the bracelet with a particular weave or knot. Outdoor, hardware, and camping stores often carry a large assortment of the cord in an array of colors. Prices are low enough that I buy hundreds of feet of the cord in a wide variety of colors. Some folks prefer garish greens, pinks, and oranges; I keep an assortment of earth tones on hand as well.

Though the idea behind the "survival bracelet" among hardcore outdoor enthusiasts is a way to keep the cord handy in case of an emergency, making the bracelets also instills a sense of belonging among members in a group. In many instances, they decide upon a color theme that identifies them as a family or a group. The activity isn't limited to bracelets: Once campers have mastered the weave—and there are dozens of patterns—they often go on to create lanyards for camp tools, car keys, camera straps, even belts. At the very least, it's useful to have a good supply of the cord on hand for making improvements around camp.

Survival bracelets teach skills and promote a sense of belonging among campers in the family or group.

FISHING

In nearly any state with water, fishing ranks among the top camping activities. If you intend to incorporate fishing into your camping experience, first inquire about regulations with the respective state or federal fish and game department. It is doubly important to learn the regulations if you are a nonresident of the state in which you intend to camp. How much fishing time, how much success, and other bounty to be gleaned from angling depends heavily on your family

Campers who add fishing to their activities can enjoy both serenity and a learning curve as they study the wily ways of fish.

structure. If you are a couple with young children, the amount of time anybody's lure spends in the water will most probably be a fraction of what you envisioned when you planned fishing as part of your trip.

The lesson here is that if you plan to fish with an emphasis on actually catching fish, be prepared for an alternative experience—and a rewarding one at that. With children ages 3 to 5, find a slender stick about 3 feet long, tie a string of about the same length at its tip, then tie on a rubber or soft plastic lure without hooks at the opposite end. Kids will spend hours on the shore, flinging their lures into the water via the homemade fishing poles. Watch them as they develop motor skills and learn about momentum. Within minutes they'll capitalize on the length of the pole, its line, and the weight of the lure to achieve the maximum casting distance with the setup. Tangles are simple to cure with the short fishing rig, and parents can take comfort knowing they won't be making a side trip to a local emergency room to have surgeons remove hooks from precious eyes, a nose, ears, cheeks, fingers, or other appendages.

For children age 6 and up, be prepared to embrace a new realm. Something clicks in the brain at that age, and it's all about accomplishment and mastery. If catching fish ranks near the top of your activities list, you've got good company. Many big-box and convenience stores sell entry-level fishing gear, including closed-face spinning reel combo rigs. (Use that exact terminology and sales associates will lead you to what you need to get your young anglers into afford-able, reliable, tangle-free fishing systems.)

If you've never fished and your kids want in, you're on equal ground when it comes to the learning curve. Though it's commendable for parents to pass on lifelong fishing skills to their children, learning to fish together as neophytes will more than reward the camping family in terms of bonding.

STARGAZING

There are 24 hours in a day, and night holds vast rewards for campers want-ing to experience the universe. Pull out a sleeping pad, lie on your back, and let the vastness sink in. The stars themselves can entertain a group for hours. Those who want to learn the names, locations, and mytholog-ical stories of stars, planets, and con-stellations can use phone apps that, held overhead, will label the constel-lations you're seeing.

Imagine for a moment that you are crossing a vast ocean and rely-ing on celestial bodies as your only means of navigation. In the Northern Hemisphere, look for the Big Dipper and draw an imaginary line extend-ing from the square end of the dip-per (opposite the handle) upward to a bright star known as Polaris. That's also known as the North Star, and the angle formed between it and the horizon denotes your lati-

It's an infinite world up there, one of awe and beauty—and it's all yours as a camper when skies are clear and you look up at night.

tude. Knowing the position of stars and their angles in the sky can also tell you the time. (Orion shines into my bedroom window, and when the Earth spins far enough that it lines up with a particular mountain peak, I know it's time to get up and start my winter day.)

BICYCLES

Bicycling has become a favorite camping activity, especially for families other-wise constrained to riding in small areas in urban settings near their homes. Many states have purchased easements and dedicated land to create extensive biking trails. Some form large loops around scenic recreation areas; others span the entire breadth of a state. Minnesota's Paul Bunyan State Trail offers an asphalt thoroughfare that runs for more than 119 miles along a reclaimed railroad. Other states offer similar venues, with smooth surfaces for wheelchairs, in-line skates, and other nonmotorized travel. Western states offer a mix of paved trails and challenging gravel or dirt mountain biking trail systems.

Whether you're riding on smooth ground or rough, helmets are a must (and may be required by law), and don't forget to pack along protective pants, shirts, and gloves. Reflectors on both your bike and clothing, along with lighting and a headlamp, are paramount for trips where you might be out in the dark.

Expect to share these trails with other riders, and inquire as to local etiquette when yielding to other modes of transportation, including folks on horseback.

If you plan to put on big miles, a basic tool kit and tire repair kit, sold at most bike shops, goes a long way to keep you pedaling instead of pushing.

Don't have bikes? Or have bikes at home but no means to haul them to the campground? Search the web for vendors who rent them out near your camping area. They'll have everything from bikes to helmets to panniers and more. They'll supply maps and recommend trails tailored to your riding ability. For adults, vendors in some states even offer bicycle-powered wine tours. (They follow with a support van, haul cases of your purchased wine, and have got you covered if the tasting gets out of hand and you need a designated driver.)

Ski resorts, particularly in the western states, have augmented their off-season by offering downhill mountain biking adventures in summer (there are beginner, intermediate, and advanced courses). You rent bikes you could never afford to

Many states offer miles of paved bike trails that connect with campgrounds.

own—with extremely awesome tires and suspensions—hang them on designated hooks on the back of the chairlift, ride to the top of the mountain, then go for an exhilarating downhill ride toward the chalet. You'll see birds and wildlife on the way up, white-knuckle your way down. Repeat the process until your forearms and calves can't take it anymore.

SWIMMING, BOATING, AND WATER SPORTS

Nothing adds an extra dimension to the camping experience quite like water. Whether it's a pond, a lake, a stream, the ocean—or a swimming pool—chances are good that you'll be spending the majority of your time near, on, or in the water. Some vendors near public campgrounds or within private campgrounds offer guided tours or other waterborne activities. They may turn you loose with watercraft rentals that range from powerboats to paddleboats, gargantuan floating tricycles, paddleboards, kayaks, canoes, rafts, inner tubes, and everything in between.

Kids love watercraft and splashing around. Make sure to set them up with properly fitted personal flotation devices for maximum safety.

Lifejackets or other personal flotation devices (PFDs) are a must near water, as is acquiring knowledge about rapids or waterfalls in a river or stream, tides on the ocean, and rain squalls on large lakes.

Though the ages and ranges of competencies in water skills may vary widely among individuals in your family, swimming usually fits all. Remember to pack your suits, towels, sandals, an umbrella, and sunscreen—and bug repellent. Biting insects dwell near most bodies of water, and local knowledge of mosquitoes and biting flies can be invaluable in choosing when to head to the water for a dip. Though most swimming areas post rules in bold letters on wooden placards or other well-marked signs, two time-proven adages will never fail you:

> Never swim alone.
> Stay within the designated swim zone markers.

Tubing is another fun activity near campgrounds with slow-moving streams. Services will drop you off with an inner tube far upstream of the camping area

CHARLIE GOES CAMPING

One of our favorite childhood activities took place each night in the tent before we shut off the lantern and zipped up our bags. We'd go around the tent, each of us naming species within a natural theme until we couldn't think of any more. We called out the names of fish, moved on to butterflies, then trees and plants, fishing lures—brands of outboard motors. With all seven of us in the game, it paid to have a few extras in mind in case a sibling called out the one we'd been ready to contribute before it was our turn. We'd exhaust our knowledge, and often there would be fewer of us with each round as we drifted off to sleep. Some nights we all digressed to giggling about who knows what. Dad would get up and shut off the gas lantern; as its flame dwindled, I would fall asleep laughing.

then pick you up at the haul-out zone, sometimes hours later. These float trips can be both memorable and relaxing.

SLACKLINING

This has become a camp favorite among adolescents, teens, and adults alike. Some campgrounds may offer ropes courses, climbing walls, or other challenges, but for cheap kicks around camp, you can pack along your own nylon climbing web, a couple of metal rings or carabiners, and a pair of trekking poles to provide an ongoing source of fun. To make the slacklining experience inviting to folks with varying degrees of balance, try stringing the webbing mere inches off the ground and offer to place "spotters" (other family members or friends to keep them from falling) on either side as they attempt to walk across the narrow, wobbly webbing like a circus tightrope walker. Those who have a bit more experience and want to master their skills often elect to use the trekking poles instead of a spotter.

Games like cribbage and "99" teach kids to add numbers fast in their heads and have fun at the same time.

CHAPTER 9

RAINY-DAY GAMES AND ACTIVITIES

A GOOD PART of my life as a family camper demands that I be part entertainer. Even when best plans have been laid for the day, like a tour of a gemstone mine or a trip to a site that offers ziplining across a canyon, there are slack moments back at camp. Though these snippets of hang time might seem glorious to us parents, kids have much less tolerance for any period of time without action.

There's a vast battery of ideas with which to entertain yourself while camping, but the trick to instigating a barrel of fun in the camp setting is to involve the whole group.

Rainy days can be tough—particularly for families with young kids—but there are plenty of activities to be done despite inclement weather. Not that cramming a bunch of folks into a tight space in unfavorable weather doesn't sometimes create a bit of crankiness—especially during rainy spells that last for days on end. But capitalizing on games or activities that bring us closer together often translates to the good stuff as the years wear on. That's the beauty of camping: providing an environment that makes us captive to one another and to our imaginations.

From making friendship bracelets to knot skill demonstrations, from journaling to playing card games, read on for proven options to keep everyone at camp occupied, laughing, and warm inside.

"I'M GOING ON A PICNIC"

There are many renditions of this game, which is great for laughter when played as a round with a circle of friends and family around the fire. The premise, as the leader of the game, is to introduce a pattern that others must decipher before they are allowed to attend your hypothetical picnic. Though secret patterns vary, one of the most popular has been to use words with double vowels or consonants.

For instance: "I'm going on a picnic and I'm bringing a yellow ball." The double *L*s qualify the rule. If the next person around the circle says, "I'm going to a picnic and I'm bringing a shallow pool," the leader says that person is invited. It may take a few rounds before other players catch on to the theme, and it becomes great fun as folks struggle with obvious ingredients such as "picnic blanket" or "ketchup."

Other renditions of the picnic game have certain colors as the secret theme, such as bringing a "red wagon," a "radish," or a "tomato."

If the group around your campfire is composed of folks who don't know one another by name, try playing a name-game variation first. This version starts with the leader stating his or her name and then adding something he or she would bring on the picnic. For example: "I'm Alice and I'm bringing mustard." The next person in line introduces himself as Jake and says he's bringing hot dog buns, perhaps. He then repeats Alice's name and tells the group that she's bringing mustard. The game is a hoot, and the last one in line has to remember all the names and the picnic supplies affixed to those names. But they also hear the repetition among the other players more than anyone else.

MAFIA

The game Mafia remains a favorite among teens and adults. Some versions use a standard deck of playing cards to establish the good guys, the bad guy, the sheriff, the blackmailer, the witness, and so on. Other renditions are played basically the same—identifying the bad guy—and include ornate cards that assign specific traits or powers to the various characters. Instruction guides are available online for generic versions of the game, and a copy of the rules usually accompanies the specialty versions sold in game and toy stores. The game often lasts several rounds and promises sufficient entertainment far into the night. The fun of each round of the game often escalates near the end when the characters remaining alive must identify the villain or the killer in the Mafia. There will be plenty of theatrical finger-pointing among the characters, actors wearing their best poker faces, and other antics as the true culprit tries to remain undiscovered.

I SPY

Simple setups often bring long-lasting laughter as intimacy grows among group members or families crowded in a tent or hunkered under a tarp in foul weather. In each round of the game I Spy, players take turns identifying an object without disclosing what they're looking at to the rest of the group. The leader begins with "I spy" then finishes the sentence with a vague clue, such as "something shiny." As players bombard the leader with errant guesses, subsequent clues to the group may be required. "It's attached to a piece of leather." The player to correctly identify that you're describing a belt buckle becomes the next leader and so on, until everybody's had a chance to spy. For even more fun with this game in large-group settings, secretly pack along miniature figurines or small objects, such as little troll dolls, tiny unicorns, and other strange objects that can be hung among socks on a clothesline or set upon stumps, stools, or cots in the tent. Instead of saying "I spy," introduce the concept with a vague comment along the lines of "I see something that doesn't fit the pattern with other things in this tent." Here's a setup hint: Tiny details often bring huge laughs. A penny lying among pairs of sandals on the floor of the tent becomes fair game, but tiny troll dolls placed on the outside of the tent, looking in through the bug screen, usually get adults laughing and youngsters curious about what else might be out of place or not quite in sync with the contents of the camp.

"UN-NATURE" TRAIL

An outdoor version of the I Spy game takes a bit of setup in advance but brings plenty of laughs with a really cool nature lesson at its end. It helps to think of it as a scavenger hunt of sorts. Ahead of time, and out of sight of others in the group, walk along a wooded section of less than 100 yards on a hiking trail and hang small troll dolls, tennis and golf balls, silk butterflies, fishing lures, a Christmas ornament or two, and other oddities from the limbs of low trees or shrubs. Bring an index card and pencil to make a map of what you put where, as you'll have to retrieve all these unnatural oddities when the game is over. As you make your way down the trail, take the time to hang objects on the back sides of large trees

Gather family and friends to find objects you've hidden.

and buried slightly under leaves on the trail. An artificial flower or two placed in the woods is another interesting addition. The object of the setup is to add a dozen or so objects that don't fit in the ecosystem. Place an obvious object in the middle of the trail to mark the end of the course.

Gather your family, friends—or both—who have no idea what's in store. Give each of them a pencil and index card. Explain that they are going on an un-nature walk and tell them to write down as many foreign objects as they can find. Encourage them to take their time, to imagine that they are an animal living in the particular stretch of woods. They should write down any oddities they see on their short walk. When they get to the end of the designated trail, have them discuss what they saw and ask them to elaborate on how many objects they found that didn't fit the theme of the forest or meadow. Expect answers to vary widely. You can divulge the exact number of objects, which often surprises most participants and makes them eager to find the objects they missed on the first pass. Ask them to walk the trail in reverse, back to the starting point, and reassess. If the activity goes well, it's an eye-opener, with lessons that increase our senses of observation when we visit the wild world. Participants usually spot the objects on the back sides of the trees and others they missed during their initial trip down the trail, but they also approach the woods with a heightened sense of observation. Adults often confide that this game reminds them of their assumptions in other realms of life.

SPLASH!

This group game relies on a 49-square grid drawn in sand, snow, mud, or other medium. The goal of the activity is for the players to communicate and discover a pattern of squares (icebergs) in which they are safe to pass from one end of the grid to the other. As the facilitator, you will have to secretly map out a pattern ahead of time that establishes the rule. A player who steps into an incorrect square has fallen into the frigid waters—*splash!*—and must go to the back of the line and try again. The key to succeeding in the game is concentration, and contestants are challenged to remember their own mistakes and those of others to deduce which squares are icebergs that will eventually lead to safe passage and solution of the puzzle. For younger participants, the course is often laid out with a simple pattern to ensure a higher rate of success. Some groups will want more challenge, so draw out several different (secret) diagrams as your key so that you can change up each round of the game.

SHERPA WALK (AKA PHOTOGRAPH)

This activity relies on a bit of physical trust and provides a fun way for groups or families to reflect upon their experiences near the end of a camping trip. For the setup, spool out the analogy that seasoned mountain climbers and explorers often place their ultimate trust in their Sherpas. Then ask them to imagine making their ascent or journey without the gift of sight—they must rely upon their Sherpas. You can use blindfolds, but having participants close their eyes works even better, as it alleviates the need for props. Sherpa Walk is one of those activities in which cheating ruins the whole game.

To play the game, have campers pair up; then instruct them to think of something tangible that represents a high point or means something special about the trip. A fishing pole or a fishing lure, for example, could represent the excitement of a camper catching his first fish. As the game ensues, participants should not divulge to anyone else what their object is. Next tell one of the partners in each pair to close his or her eyes. Now the Sherpa, whose eyes remain open, leads the (blind) camper carefully away from the campfire or the bench to the object that represents an experience. When the pair has arrived at the object, the Sherpa instructs the camper to open his or her eyes and points to the object of meaning. The Sherpa and the blind camper exchange roles and repeat the process.

When everyone has switched roles and returned to the main campsite, it's time to find out where the Sherpas took the travelers, what they found, and what the object means to them.

MAGICAL UTENSILS

For this crowd baffler you will need a metal fork, a metal spoon, a wooden match, and a glass jar or drinking glass. You can bend the inner tines of the fork slightly so that they pinch the broad end of the spoon as you gently push the two pieces of silverware together. Now take the wooden match and position its unlit end between the two center tines of the fork. Adjust the match for balance then place the assembly so that the whole works hangs precariously over the outside of the glass. If you've assembled things correctly, the unlit head of the

This activity challenges our understanding of balance. Watch as the end of the match burns back and leaves the remainder precariously perched on the rim of the glass.

match should protrude toward the inside of the glass, with the remaining section supporting the silverware outside the rim. Here comes the fun part: With another match, light the head of the balancing match. Watch it burn. Will it fall? As a caveat, this games works best without wind.

CHOPSTICKS

This low-energy finger tapping game takes a little time to learn, but the fun escalates quickly, and the game becomes a mainstay as players learn to strategize their moves and touch the fingers of their opponents to take them out of the game. To play, two opponents face each other with the index finger of each hand extended. They agree which player will start the game, which doesn't add any appreciable advantage in the greater scope of the game. The starting player (A) takes one finger of either hand and taps the opposing player (B), who then must add and extend another finger and hold out two fingers on the hand that was tapped. Player B then takes a turn and may choose to tap the fingers of player A with the two fingers, which requires player A to hold out three. Now the danger begins. Player A can use the three fingers of the one hand to tap the hand where player B holds out two fingers, for a total of five, which takes that hand out of the game. In one of the more common versions of the rules, player B can redeem a dead hand by bumping two hands together to form three fingers on each hand, which becomes formidable ammunition against player A. Once players are familiar with the rules and the pace of the game, it's fun to invite third and fourth players.

Chopsticks and other simple hand games provide a great way to fill idle times at camp.

CARD GAMES

Break out a new card game. Campers might be tired of Uno but in the mood for Crazy 8s, a game of 99, or myriad other card games that can be learned quickly. Or learn to play cribbage, a card game synonymous with Alaska's remote mining and fishing camps. Though you can use a pencil and paper to track scores, campers with a lot of time on their hands often end up drilling a board with 122 holes and using matchsticks for pegs. The boards are inexpensive to buy at game or hobby stores, and the game lends itself to homeschooling or teaching kids math

in the abstract form as the cards become flash cards. If you play the game often, they'll get lightning fast at combining numbers that add up to 15 and 31.

ROCK, PAPER, SCISSORS EXTREME

The tried-and-true Rock, Paper, Scissors game takes on a new dimension with large groups in which participants pair off and all start at the same time. Players randomly pair off, running through the sequence until one of them wins. The winner then challenges the winner of another pair to another round. Meanwhile, the loser of the first round becomes the winner's private cheering section. The respective cheerleaders follow the winner of that round to the next round, and the game culminates with the final two contestants challenging each other, each with his or her own large cheering section. This is great icebreaker for large-scale camps, and the more players the better. Though the game doesn't generate a lot of energy in groups of six or fewer, twenty players have a lot of fun, and one hundred players is not too many.

Cute critters often become the characters of children's bedtime stories in camp.

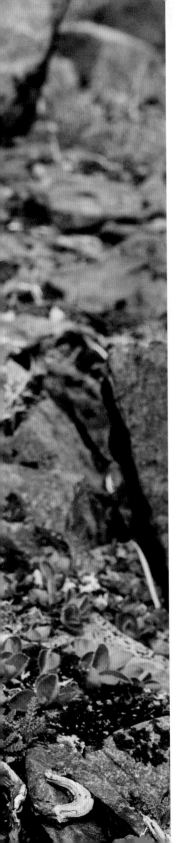

CHAPTER 10

CAMPFIRE STORIES

FOR ME, stories and story structure make up the rhythm of life. Teachers told us back in grade school that all stories need a beginning, middle, and end. More recently we hear about the setup, the conflict, and the resolution in an attempt to grasp a better understanding of elements that compose the dramatic arc. That dramatic arc, by the way, lures us into finishing just about every book, watching every TV show or movie. And stories detailing the fabric of our lives are told everywhere—in airports and grocery stores checkout lines; at meetings, school, and church.

JOKES

In their simplest forms, stories are told as jokes:

A weasel walks into a cafe, sits down at a table, and waits for service. The waiter walks to the table, looks over the edge, and sees the tiny weasel on the chair below.

The waiter goes, "I've never served meals to a weasel before."

Pop goes the weasel. Incorporating critters you've seen by day into the characters of campfire stories at night instills the drama inspired by the natural world.

And the weasel goes, "You got something against weasels?"

"No," says the waiter after a long pause. "What will it be?"

"Pop," goes the weasel.

IMPORTANT ELEMENTS OF STORYTELLING

The best stories may seem effortlessly told, but look closer and you'll see that they all feature well-crafted setup and execution. Here are a few things you can do to tell the best campfire story.

Build Suspense

Camping offers the perfect setting for good stories, especially at night, when inky black darkness adds the dramatic element of the unseen. There's always something out there, right? And don't we all pine for that perennial favorite beginning of the drama when someone suddenly breaks his or her gaze from the glow of the campfire to the darkness behind:

"What was that?"

"What was what?"

(We've got the attention of our audience now.)

"That! Did you hear it, like the sound of heavy breathing?"

(Bam! They're hooked for a long night of storytelling.)

An obligatory consideration of the storyteller would be the age and temperament of the audience. The above approach to setting the stage works only when everybody in the group is game. We want positive, long-lasting memories of our outings in the woods—not nightmares. So many times we've used the hours around nightly campfires as the catalyst to stories of haunted forests, mythical beasts, and unsolved mysteries. But we keep a passel of comforting stories up our sleeves for those who are young, gullible, or new to the experience of a night out in the woods. In fact, I often incorporate little kids into manufacturing campfire stories based upon their experiences of the day.

As for ingredients, most younger children have been steeped in animated movies with themes of puppies or kittens that are living less-than-savory lives in animal shelters. In most cases the abandoned pets wind up with loving owners who scoop them up and offer a good home forever after. Crafting your own version of a story that competes with the big screen might seem a tall order to fill. Fear not. You, as storyteller, don't have to get there all in one night. Try fabricating longer stories in 10- or 20-minute episodes. Begin each night with a recap

"Did you hear that strange noise?"

CHARLIE GOES CAMPING

We had set up a tent in the yard for the granddaughters to play in all summer long, and though we slept out only two nights that I can remember, the camp setting proved priceless. On one of our days playing in the yard, the little girls and I had the great fortune of meeting (for real) a small field mouse, who apparently camped in the flower beds festooning the foundation of the house.

On numerous afternoons the girls and I watched as the little critter scurried across the gravel driveway and disappeared into the tall grasses where it foraged. One particular afternoon, the mouse began its return across the driveway toward the flower beds; I instructed the girls to stand very still. We stood in awe as the little mouse not only came straight toward us but climbed on Riley's sandaled foot, spun around to survey its surroundings, then darted into a dense patch of pansies.

It was a peak experience for the girls and me. That night we named the little mouse Punt and incorporated the newly celebrated rodent into all our bedtime stories for weeks to come.

of where you left off the night before, and take your sweet time building on the middle of Act II, the heart of the conflict, where prospects of a better home for the little kitties and puppies look grim.

Or scrap the Hollywood themes and come up with a story all your own. Younger children often will want to pack a stuffed animal or two along with their camping gear, and those animals can become awesome characters in the creation of a campfire story. Another trick is to incorporate birds and animals you've seen as a family into the stories. You emerge from the tent in the morning to hear the piercing call of a blue jay. The kids will remember that, especially if you center their attention on the beautiful bird. And luckily for the storyteller, that bird comes packed with drama; there are hawks and other predators about the woods, and the bird must ensure that its offspring are safe from those predators and have ample shelter and food. Good stuff for the night ahead.

Live the Story

As you and your family assimilate formative experiences at your camps, the story structure will fall into place. You arise in the morning. You eat breakfast. You talk about the upcoming day's activities. Or you say little, slam down your breakfast, and head off into the hills. In either scenario, that's the setup, the Act I for tonight's story. What follows, what unfolds in even the most mundane day of camping, is an unavoidable Act II. In drama, this is where the hero meets and attempts to overpower the villain or other forces that form conflict or intense challenge. In the story structure of camping, this will be the steep rocky trail, the whitecaps that suddenly formed on the lake, the momentary hang time of a close encounter with a bear. The campers as main characters make choices, and

CHARLIE GOES CAMPING

We wanted to paddle to the far side of a large lake. The wind came up, but we thought we could make it to the protection of the far shore. That was the plan, after all, the purpose of the trip. Our research indicated great camping spots there. Choices. The wind came up a couple notches more. Then we got scared. We pushed on, nerves racked by the large waves crashing against a rocky shore. When it seemed things couldn't get any worse, we spotted an opening in the rocks, the entrance to a sheltered cove. We paddled into its calm waters, hauled out the canoes, and discovered a clear-water stream, lush plant life, and birds like we'd never seen.

The wind squall abated; the whitecaps disappeared. We resumed paddling toward our goal, the far shore, only to discover crowds of other campers, many of whom were intoxicated. That discovery threw us into the next choice, and it provided movement into Act III. It was nearing nightfall, but the winds were calm. We turned the canoes around and paddled all the way back to spend the next three days in the tranquility of our newfound cove.

Though the above story is a composite of several of my camping trips on Alaska's large lakes, every trip has had its twists and turns and has challenged me. On one of these outings, while we waited for the large waves to dissipate, Cheryl walked into the woods along a small creek and discovered a recreational cabin. On its porch she found a shovel and a gold pan. You guessed it: We spent the afternoon panning and actually found several small nuggets of gold—not a bad Act III, if you ask me.

When I make camp with others for the night, I instigate the storytelling by summarizing the beginning of our day. Within moments, others begin to contribute details that make up the high and low points of our day in drama.

like any good movie, those choices lead to action. Action leads to movement—and the revelation to ourselves who we are, what we're made of. Those elements propel us down an irreversible path of growth, of rich transformation that camping so amply provides.

AND/BUT

In family settings where siblings have entered their teenage years, storytelling often morphs into a group experience. A favorite impromptu storytelling setup is to initiate a game I learned as "And/But." This technique works best if everyone sits in a circle. The rules for the first round are that everyone tries to take a turn building upon the part of the story they most recently heard. With the exception of the person starting the game, all the players have to start their first line with the word "but."

Here's an example:

"I went to the well this morning."

The next person in line says, "But the well was dry."

The next person builds with something like "But I didn't need water anyway."

The story continues until it reaches the facilitator or whoever began the story.

In the next round, players build a brand-new story or expand on the one from the previous round. This time, however, the players must all begin with the word "and." Invariably this round goes much easier, as the word "and" pushes the momentum in the story fragments forward more quickly than the word "but," which is often associated with a hurdle. Besides the hilarious stories, the exercise sometimes challenges players to reframe how they talk to one another.

Telling a joke or recounting a funny experience from along the trail often gets campfire stories rolling long into the night.

CHARLIE GOES CAMPING

One summer I led a crew of five on a service project to improve hiking trails in one of Alaska's state parks. A recurrent theme in the drama of our days became the absence of firewood. We'd scrounged twigs, small sticks, and other fuel in our travels throughout the day, but the blaze didn't last nearly as long into the night as we'd hoped.

The other conflict centered on a particular girl who, above all, wanted to see a bear on this trip. Though they are rampant in the area on most summer nights, and the hiking trails were riddled with scat, we hadn't seen a bear in nearly four days on the trail.

Eventually our trail work took us to the shore of a large glacial lake. There we discovered a vast furrow of dried driftwood that had been washed up along the shoreline. It had been a long day, but after returning to camp, another camper and I set off on a return mission, hiking the mile or so back to the lake with empty frame packs and short ropes. With the abundant supply of wood available, we could afford to be selective in choosing the best sticks and logs. We returned with our packs bulging with enough wood to keep our fires burning for two more nights.

On the last night before we were to pack up our camp and hike out, the girl announced that she'd head to the lake alone to get a load of firewood. Though I usually suggest and uphold the buddy system of at least two people traveling together in the backcountry, I sensed that her solo journey was imperative to her sense of self-discovery. Clearly this was a character-making choice.

She went. She collected firewood—and she saw a bear on the way back to camp.

"You can go down to the lake and play, but only if your older brother is watching you.

Or: "Ask your older brother if he'll take you down to the lake and play."

It's all in the packaging.

Pack along a guitar or other musical instruments for prime-time entertainment after sundown.

CHAPTER 11

CLASSIC CAMPFIRE SONGS

CAMPFIRE SONGS may transport us back to some of the oldest tunes in history, and their origins are muddled in political and sometimes not-so-optimistic socioeconomic times. Strangely enough, songs about frogs that go looking for a mate, kitchen utensils that elope, and horses that are too old to pull a plow yet go on to set speed records in trotting events ("Old Gray Mare") have not only survived through the years but also remain the tunes sung around campfires today. There are many regional or colloquial variations of the lyrics in each of the songs shared below.

If you're not sure of the melodies, check online for videos to get you on track, not only with the melodies but also with the associated actions that accompany many of these songs.

Additionally, you can trust kids to put wild spins on the lyrics and modify the songs to become their own. Though "Jingle Bells" has been associated with Christmas, crazy variations involving Batman, Robin, and the Joker remain favorites of kids camping in summer.

This song has obscure roots dating back to the mid-1800s and may have evolved from an event in which a 10-year-old mare set a trotting record—an unusual feat for a horse of that age. The song contradicts itself in the second verse, where the old mare still has enough spunk to kick out at the whiffletree, a heavy wooden pole designed to sit crossways and separate the heavy leather harness traces a few feet behind the horse. The song was recorded by several artists, including Bing Crosby, in the early 1900s. I learned it when I was about 5 years old.

Oh the old gray mare,
She ain't what she used to be,
Ain't what she used to be,
Ain't what she used to be.
The old gray mare,
She ain't what she used to be,
Many long years ago.

Oh the old gray mare,
She kicked on the whiffletree,
Kicked on the whiffletree,
Kicked on the whiffletree.
The old gray mare,
She kicked on the whiffletree,
Many long years ago.

Many long years ago,
Many long years ago,
The old gray mare,
She ain't what she used to be,
Many long years ago.

Many long years ago,
Many long years ago,
The old gray mare,
She kicked on the whiffletree,
Many long years ago.

Joining in song by the campfire is a wonderful activity for the whole family.

A longtime favorite at Scout camps and camps catering to large groups, this song often emerges around the campfire each summer. Like many camping songs, this one comes with actions that range from wiggling fingers to signify the twig, raising an arm for the limb, and so on. In a wild variation, a hippopotamus winds up on top of the flea near the end for an extra silly round.

Ho, ro, the rattlin' bog,
The bog down in the valley-o.
Ho, ro, the rattlin' bog,
The bog down in the valley-o.

In that bog there was a tree,
A rare tree, a rattlin' tree;
The tree in the bog,
In the bog down in the valley-o.

Ho, ro, the rattlin' bog,
The bog down in the valley-o.
Ho, ro, the rattlin' bog,
The bog down in the valley-o.

And on that tree there was a limb,
A rare limb, a rattlin' limb;
The limb on the tree,
And the tree in the bog,
In the bog down in the valley-o.

Ho, ro, the rattlin' bog,
The bog down in the valley-o.
Ho, ro, the rattlin' bog,
The bog down in the valley-o.

And on that limb there was a branch,
A rare branch, a rattlin' branch;
The branch on the limb,
The limb on the tree,
And the tree in the bog,
In the bog down in the valley-o.

Ho, ro, the rattlin' bog,
The bog down in the valley-o.
Ho, ro, the rattlin' bog,
The bog down in the valley-o.

And on that branch there was a twig,
A rare twig, a rattlin' twig;
The twig on the branch,
The branch on the limb,
The limb on the tree,
And the tree in the bog,
In the bog down in the valley-o.

Ho, ro, the rattlin' bog,
The bog down in the valley-o,
Ho, ro, the rattlin' bog,
The bog down in the valley-o.

And on that twig there was a nest,
A rare nest, a rattlin' nest;
The nest on the twig,
The twig on the branch,
The branch on the limb,
The limb on the tree,
And the tree in the bog,
In the bog down in the valley-o.

Ho, ro, the rattlin' bog,
The bog down in the valley-o.
Ho, ro, the rattlin' bog,
The bog down in the valley-o.
And in that nest there was an egg,

A rare egg, a rattlin' egg;
The egg in the nest,
The nest on the twig,
The twig on the branch,
The branch on the limb,
The limb on the tree,
And the tree in the bog,
In the bog down in the valley-o.

Ho, ro, the rattlin' bog,
The bog down in the valley-o.
Ho, ro, the rattlin' bog,
The bog down in the valley-o.

And on that egg there was a bird,
A rare bird, a rattlin' bird;
The bird on the egg,
The egg in the nest,
The nest on the twig,
The twig on the branch,
The branch on the limb,
The limb on the tree,
And the tree in the bog,
In the bog down in the valley-o.

Ho, ro, the rattlin' bog,
The bog down in the valley-o.
Ho, ro, the rattlin' bog,
The bog down in the valley-o.

And on that bird there was a feather,
A rare feather, a rattlin' feather;
The feather on the bird,
The bird on the egg,
The egg in the nest,
The nest on the twig,
The twig on the branch,
The branch on the limb,
The limb on the tree,

And the tree in the bog,
In the bog down in the valley-o.
Ho, ro, the rattlin' bog,
The bog down in the valley-o.
Ho, ro, the rattlin' bog,
The bog down in the valley-o.

And on that feather there was a flea,
A rare flea, a rattlin' flea;
The flea in the feather,
The feather on the bird,
The bird on the egg,
The egg in the nest,
The nest on the twig,
The twig on the branch,
The branch on the limb,
The limb on the tree,
And the tree in the bog,
In the bog down in the valley-o.

Ho, ro, the rattlin' bog,
The bog down in the valley-o.
Ho, ro, the rattlin' bog,
The bog down in the valley-o.

Ho, ro, the rattlin' bog,
The bog down in the valley-o.
Ho, ro, the rattlin' bog,
The bog down in the valley-o.

Ho, ro, the rattlin' bog,
The bog down in the valley-o.
Ho, ro, the rattlin' bog,
The bog down in the valley-o.

Ho, ro, the rattlin' bog,
The bog down in the valley-o.
Ho, ro, the rattlin' bog,
The bog down in the valley-o.

"THE HOLE"

Very similar to "Rattlin' Bog," this song puts an elephant on top of the flea.

There was a hole,
The prettiest little hole that you ever
    did see.
And the hole was in the ground,
And the green grass grew all around
    and around,
And the green grass grew all around.
    [clap clap]

And in that hole, there was a tree,
The prettiest little tree that you ever
    did see.
And the tree was in the hole,
And the hole was in the ground,
And the green grass grew all around
    and around,
And the green grass grew all around.
    [clap clap]

(Repeat and add on:)
On the tree, branch;
On the branch, twig;
On the twig, nest;
In the nest, egg;
On the egg, bird;
On the bird, wing;
On the wing, feather;
On the feather, flea;
On the flea, elephant;

(Last verse)
And on that flea there was an
    elephant,
The prettiest little elephant that you
    ever did see.
And the elephant was on the flea,
And the flea was on the feather,
And the feather was on the wing,
And the wing was on the bird,
And the bird was on the egg,
And the egg was in the nest,
And the nest was on the twig,
And the twig was on the branch,
And the branch was on the tree,
And the tree was in the hole,
And the hole was in the ground,
And the green grass grew all around
    and around,
And the green grass grew all around.

"LITTLE BUNNY FOO FOO"

This camp song was first introduced to us at a rendezvous after a long winter of camping with our dog teams back in the 1980s. The melody lends itself to action and has been borrowed from the 1948 song "Down by the Station," which has the same melody as the French Canadian tune "Alouette," written in 1879.

Little Bunny Foo Foo hopping
    through the forest,
Scooping up the field mice and
    bopping 'em on the head.
Down came the good fairy and she
    said:
"Little Bunny Foo Foo, I don't want to
    see you
"Scooping up the field mice and
    bopping 'em on the head.
"I'll give you three more chances and
    if you don't behave,
"I'm going to turn you into a goon!"
So the next day . . .
Little Bunny Foo Foo hopping
    through the forest,
Scooping up the field mice and
    bopping 'em on the head.
Down came the good fairy and she
    said:
"Little Bunny Foo Foo, I don't want to
    see you
"Scooping up the field mice and
    bopping 'em on the head.
"I'll give you two more chances and if
    you don't behave,
"I'm going to turn you into a goon!"
So the next day . . .

Little Bunny Foo Foo hopping
    through the forest,
Scooping up the field mice and
    bopping 'em on the head.
Down came the good fairy and she
    said:
"Little Bunny Foo Foo, I don't want to
    see you
"Scooping up the field mice and
    bopping 'em on the head.
"I'll give you one more chances and if
    you don't behave,
"I'm going to turn you into a goon!"
So the next day . . .
Little Bunny Foo Foo hopping
    through the forest,
Scooping up the field mice and
    bopping 'em on the head.
Down came the good fairy and she
    said:
"I gave you three chances and you
    didn't behave;
"Now I'm going to turn you into a
    goon!"
Moral of the story is . . .
"Hare today, goon tomorrow!"

"LITTLE GREEN FROG SONG"

Like many camp songs, this one comes with actions that accompany each verse to make it more fun. When you sing the first "mm," blink your eyes. On the second "mm" stick out your tongue. When you come to the part where you sing "la-di-da-di-da," clap once then spread your arms and wiggle your little frog fingers. The melody for this song has been loosely borrowed from another old-time song, "Old Gray Mare," which was about a horse who remained uncharacteristically athletic at 10 years old. Lyrics vary across the globe; another version has the little green frog saying "galumph" in place of "mm."

"Mm mm" went the little green frog
    one day,
"Mm mm" went the little green frog,
"Mm mm" went the little green frog
    one day;
So they all went "mm mm, ah!"
But we know frogs go "la-di-da-di-da,
"la-di-da-di-da, la-di-da-di-da."
We know frogs go "la-di-da-di-da";
They don't go "mm mm, ah!"

"GREASY, GRIMY GOPHER GUTS"

This was my first camp song, believe it or not, taught to me at the age of around 5. Funny how indelible the lyrics remain in my mind and can be recalled some fifty-eight years later. This melody also follows that of the "Old Gray Mare," but more closely than the "Little Green Frog Song."

Great big bowls of greasy, grimy
    gopher guts,
Marinated monkey meat,
Vultures vomit at your feet;
French-fried eyeballs
Floatin' in a pool of blood,
And me without a spoon.

Many songs have accompanying motions that add to the fun in a large group.

MEATBALLS AND SPAGHETTI
(SUNG TO THE TUNE OF "ON TOP OF OLD SMOKEY")

The melody of this song is derived from an old folk song, "On Top of Old Smokey," about waiting too long to court a lover. Though there is no shortage of sardonic verses online about deceitful lovers, lies, and other mayhem that lead to loneliness and loss, this is the version we remember from our childhood camp songs.

On top of spaghetti,
All covered with cheese,
I lost my poor meatball,
When somebody sneezed.

It rolled off the table
And on to the floor,
And then my poor meatball
Rolled out of the door.

It rolled in the garden
And under a bush,
And then my poor meatball
Was nothing but mush.

The mush was as tasty,
As tasty could be,
And then the next summer,
It grew into a tree.

The tree was all covered,
All covered with moss,
And on it grew meatballs
And tomato sauce.

So if you eat spaghetti,
All covered with cheese,
Hold on to your meatball
Whenever you sneeze.

A guitar or other instrument adds musical momentum to silly songs and keeps campers rolling through the verses.

"BINGO"

This preschool and kindergarten favorite continues its prolonged life when youngsters sing it around the campfire.

There were some kids who had a dog
And Bingo was his name O.
B-I-N-G-O,
B-I-N-G-O,
B-I-N-G-O,
And Bingo was his name O.

There were some kids who had a dog
And Bingo was his name O.
[Clap]-I-N-G-O,
[Clap]-I-N-G-O,
[Clap]-I-N-G-O,
And Bingo was his name O.

There were some kids who had a dog
And Bingo was his name O.
[Clap-clap]-N-G-O,
[Clap-clap]-N-G-O,
[Clap-clap]-N-G-O,
And Bingo was his name O.

There were some kids who had a dog
And Bingo was his name O.
[Clap-clap-clap]-G-O,
[Clap-clap-clap]-G-O,
[Clap-clap-clap]-G-O,
And Bingo was his name O.

There were some kids who had a dog
And Bingo was his name O.
[Clap-clap-clap-clap]-O,
[Clap-clap-clap-clap]-O,
[Clap-clap-clap-clap]-O,
And Bingo was his name O.

There were some kids who had a dog
And Bingo was his name O.
[Clap-clap-clap-clap-clap],
[Clap-clap-clap-clap-clap],
[Clap-clap-clap-clap-clap],
And Bingo was his name O.

B-I-N-G-O, B-I-N-G-O, B-I-N-G-O,
And Bingo was his name O.
Bingo was his name O,
Bingo was his name.

"HEY DIDDLE DIDDLE"

This short song originated sometime in the 1600s and stems from an artistic expression of elation and an Old World avatar that commonly showed cats playing fiddles to show that elation. The bit about the moon later evolved into the more contemporary phrase "over the moon," as in, "We're over the moon about pulling off this family camping trip!"

Hey Diddle Diddle,
The cat and the fiddle,
The cow jumped over the moon.
The little dog laughed
To see such sport,
And the dish ran away with the spoon.

Camp life is sometimes all about improvising with what you have available around you.

CAMP LIFE
HACKS

I stood in disbelief at the splintered axe handle in my hand. I had bought the tool, brand-new, at an outpost in Alaska a few days before with the intention that it would serve as my primary way of splitting wood, downing small trees, and completing myriad other chores around the camp for the next month. I raised the axe high overhead, then swung forcefully in an attempt to split an alder stump. But as the axe made contact, the hickory handle made a resounding crack.

I was 70 miles from the nearest town, and I had been transported to this particular camp by a fishing boat. My brother and I had committed to camping here for the next month. The fix? We aligned the broken pieces (as the handle had broken diagonally along the grain of the wood), grabbed a spool of heavy fishing twine, and wound more than a hundred wraps tightly around the two pieces to splice them back together. It worked! Though we abstained from trying to split the stubborn alder stump, the axe served us well for the remainder of our days in camp.

When is wire more than wire? When it's strung through the holes of two tent poles and twisted tightly in lieu of a missing nut and bolt. On winter nights, heat water to near boiling with an ultralight camping stove and pour it into your drinking bottle. Pull your socks over the bottle and take it to bed for a cozy night in the sleeping bag.

In this chapter we'll share hacks that can keep you camping when things fall apart, and offer great tricks for added camping comfort when they're not.

The double figure-eight knot

CHAPTER 12

KNOTS TO KNOW

OF ALL THE CAMPING gear we own, the most ubiquitous items around the house, in storage totes, in backpacks, and in our cars would be lengths of rope, line, twine, string, and cordage. Though the differences between these terms and their uses have been argued among sailors, loggers, anglers, and mountain climbers, think of them as the magical strands that hold together just about anything in camp. They lash poles together, hold out tents and tarps, stretch hammocks between trees, and tie down or anchor boats in a storm.

Knowledge of knots—or rope skills, as they're often called—consists of two parts: knowing which knot to use to meet your camping needs, and knowing how to tie it. While it would behoove the camper to acquire these skills well ahead of the time you need to lash something together during a storm at camp, that's rarely the way it goes. Read on for a handy guide to the knots campers need to know.

Cordage also has two parts: the standing part, the main length of the rope; and the standing end, the portion you will use to tie your knot. For ease in deciding which knot to use, we've divided them into categories: loops, hitches, knots that join separate lines, and others to get the job done. We'll also provide a guide on how to use knots in combinations to tie bikes, coolers, grills, and other large items to racks on vehicles.

LOOPS

Bowline

The bowline has won renown worldwide for its strength and the ease with which it can be undone after taking on tons of tension. The bowline as a loop won't slip or cinch down, which has won acclaim in all arenas, from mountain climbing to boating to horsemanship—you name it. Small wonder that it's a favorite of campers. To tie it, form a bend in the line near its end and throw the short end over the long end, leaving a sufficient amount of tail to form the rest of the knot. Next, use your fingers to form a loop in the long, standing section of the line so that it encloses the tail. Bring the tail around the standing part of the line below the loop then tuck it back through the loop. The length of the tail protruding from the finished knot should be approximately 10 times the line's diameter.

The time-tested bowline provides a loop that won't chafe itself under heavy strain and is easily undone.

Alpine Butterfly

If you need a loop formed quickly along the standing part of any line, you'll fall in love with the alpine butterfly. The knot can be undone easily after subjecting the line to a heavy load and won't slip in any direction. To tie the alpine butterfly, you'll need enough slack in the standing part of the line to take a wrap around four fingers of your hand. Make the first loop near your fingertips, and make two more loops in the same direction, the first of these two wraps around your fingers but at a diagonal toward your thumb. The second loop should be wrapped around the meaty section of your hand and diagonally across to form an *X* in the palm of your hand. Grab the first loop and pull over the top of the *X*, then pull it under to form a loop as you draw slack toward your fingertips. Adjust the knot so that its turns are symmetrical with the loop in the center. The alpine butterfly is our favorite loop in the mix of knots that form a trucker's hitch.

The alpine butterfly is easy to tie and forms a loop that won't slip, no matter which direction you pull from.

Figure-Eight Loop

Like the name implies, this knot resembles the number "8" when tied properly. The knot has won renown among climbers for affixing climbing rope to the harness, but it has many other uses where a secure, nonslip loop is needed. To tie the figure-eight loop, pull a large loop in the line so that it doubles, then twist the two strands of the standing part a turn and a half and stuff the remaining loop back through. Tighten and form. To tie the figure-eight loop through a fixed eye, grommet, or metal ring, you'll need to leave sufficient tail to form a loop to the size of your liking. Tie the first single figure eight, pull the tail through the metal ring, then double it back through the knot. The trick to completing the final steps in tying the knot is to keep the flow of the line parallel to the first "8" when tracing the tail back through the knot toward its standing part.

The loop formed by a double figure-eight knot will not cinch down and is the most common way of tying climbing rope to the climbing harness.

Improved Clinch Knot

This ubiquitous loop knot has been a favorite of anglers for decades for its qualities of cinching down tightly on the eyes of hooks or other fixed loops—particularly metal rings—where you want to stop all sideways slippage. To tie the knot, thread the standing end of the line through the eye of the fishhook and pull an extra 2 inches of tail back toward the standing part. Twist the standing end over the standing part five times; take the remaining tail and thread it between the space in the first twist after the eye of the hook. Holding the tail taut while cinching down the knot ensures that the wraps form consistently around the standing part. This knot cannot be undone and needs to be cut off the hook when switching to different hooks, baits, or other tackle.

Cat's Paw

This knot works wonders for securing line in an open hook so that it stays balanced and doesn't slip when lifting objects or keeping racks or poles suspended horizontally in camp. It's ideal for clothes racks, poles, or other applications suspended from a single line above. Tie it by grasping the line with both hands at a midpoint between its ends; twist your fingers symmetrically to form twists in each half of the loop. We like to use it in conjunction with carabiners and other fasteners around camp.

HITCHES

Clove Hitch

This is another favorite knot for lashing items together. Unlike the bowline and other knots that form loops, the clove hitch must be tied around an object,

The clove hitch provides a handy grip for tying to trees or lashing objects together at odd angles. Always finish off a clove hitch with a backing hitch to ensure that it won't come undone.

such as a stick, pole, or rail. To tie it, take the end and toss it away from you, over the rail or rails, with enough tail to continue about three more wraps around the pole. Next, bring the tail from under the rail toward you on the left side of the initial strand of line laid over the rails. Cross over the original strand of line and continue circling the rail in the same direction. Grab the tail from the underside of the rail and pull it toward you but on the inside (left) of your previous wrap. This knot can be tied in many ways and from multiple directions. Always tie an overhand knot by throwing the leftover standing end over the standing part. Cinch down tightly.

JOINING LINES

Square Knot

Joining two lines together effectively with a square knot—also known among sailors as the reef knot—takes less time than tying a shoe. The knot works best

when both lines are of equal diameter, and mastering the square knot requires no more than crossing the standing ends of two lines with a twist (like tying a shoe) then crossing the lines in another twist in the opposite direction. The telltale feature of a correctly tied square knot is that the beginning and end of each rope will lie parallel under the loop formed by the other. When you roll the knot over, the underside should look the same. The square knot under a lot of tension can be a beast to undo, but for light duty it is king.

The square knot provides a super-quick way to join two lines together. Leave a sufficient tail on each of the lines, as the knot will draw the tails in slightly when it tightens.

Sheet Bend

The sheet bend takes slightly more time to tie than a square knot, but it shines when it's time to undo the knot after it has been under a lot of tension. Like the inner workings of the bowline, the knot has been constructed to lock itself in place and distribute the load equally among strands of line so that it doesn't cut itself. To tie the sheet bend, pull a loop in one line, pinch the standing end to the standing part with one hand, then insert the standing end of the other through the loop in the first line and pass it back under itself so that the standing end lies perpendicular to the loop. For added strength, or when joining lines of dissimilar diameter, make two or three passes with the second, smaller-diameter line under itself. Leave a sufficient tail so that the standing end won't retract within the inner knot when tension is applied.

Like the bowline, the sheet bend won't slip under immense pressure and can be easily undone.

Water Knot

The water knot remains a favorite among mountain climbers for its attributes of safety in joining all types of lines—in particular, the flat nylon climbing web used for accessories and homemade climbing harnesses. The beauty of the water knot is that it maximizes the bearing surfaces of the joined lines or webbing, as the inner workings of the knot all lie parallel upon each other. To tie the water knot, begin with a simple overhand knot with a sufficient length of standing end. Take the rope you wish to join and begin at the protruding standing end of the first knot; trace the second line through the overhand, keeping the strands of both lines parallel. The tail, or standing end, of the second line should protrude by the same amount along the standing part of the first line at the opposite end of the knot.

Begin the water knot by tying an overhand knot in one line, then enter and trace the face the first knot with the second line from the opposite direction. The water knot is a favorite of rock climbers for joining two lines.

OTHER KNOTS

Keg Knot

If the keg knot goes by another name, we have yet to find it, but this ingenious invention can be tied and released under moderate to heavy tension. To tie the keg knot, pass the standing end of the line away from you through the loop of another line or through a metal ring. Pull the standing end toward you, crossing the first line in a hard bend, then bring it through the back side of the loop toward you. The compound bends offer huge mechanical advantage, and you can often hold tension while finishing off the knot with a series of at least four half hitches along the standing part of the line. Releasing the knot involves undoing the half hitches but holding the tail tightly in one hand while undoing the last hitch with the other. The same mechanical advantage of the line bending over itself and the other line or metal eye allows you to slip the standing end through the knot and release the tension.

The keg knot can be tied and released under light to moderate pressure. Finish off the keg knot with a series of hitches to keep it from coming undone.

Trucker's Hitch

This combination of knots to hold items securely is somewhat of a misnomer, as the trucking industry long ago evolved to heavy straps and locking load binders to secure cargo to flatbed trailers and trucks. However, the knot will never die among campers and others needing to lash down boxes, crates, bicycles, kayaks, or rafts to vehicle bumpers or racks, and it remains a favorite way to apply significant tension to tent flies and to stretch hammocks fiddle-string tight between trees. The hitch works equally well with a single length of line or multiple lines and offers creative solutions around camp. To tie the trucker's hitch, run a line between the item to lash down and a solid anchor.

For example, tie one end of a hammock to a stout tree. At the other end of the hammock, run another line from the eye of the hammock and circle a distant tree three times. Allow enough slack in the standing part to tie an alpine butterfly loop about midway

Use a trucker's hitch to tighten up a hammock between trees. The loop in this hitch is the alpine butterfly.

between the tree and the hammock. Tighten the loops around the tree. Pass the standing end of the line through the same loop in the end of the hammock, through the alpine butterfly, then back through the loop in the hammock. Reef it back. Hard. Finish it off with a clove hitch around all three strands of line protruding from the ring. Each pass of the line through a knot or the loop in the hammock multiplies the force applied.

That same mechanical efficiency can be used to move heavy objects. Tie a line between a heavy log and a large tree—you'll amaze your camping compatriots with your ingenuity and strength as the giant log lurches under your command.

OTHER HACKS USING KNOTS AND ROCKS

Even on days of favorable weather, winds can increase to make life tedious around the picnic table, especially if the corners of the tablecloth begin whipping like flags in the breeze. Here's the fix: Find four smooth stones, about the size of a golf ball or slightly smaller. Have short lengths of lightweight line handy (you might only need two). Place the smooth stone several inches inside a corner of the tablecloth and bend the cloth over the corner so that the stone is cocooned in the fabric. Tuck in the excess material. Grab the rock and begin twisting so that it's contained tightly within the cocoon. Take the twine and tie a clove hitch tightly around the twisted material immediately behind the stone. Finish it off with an overhand knot. Repeat the process for the other three corners. Depending on the geometry of the picnic table, you might be able to reach across under the bottom of the planks and tie the two tails of twine together with a square

CHARLIE GOES CAMPING

If it's rocks you're lacking, packing a lucky penny or two—or more—in your camping gear can save the day when sudden winds whip up and rip your tarp or rainfly.

I was recently eating breakfast with a good friend and sharing camping experiences. He asked me if I'd heard the adage "Bring your lucky pennies" as applied to camping and a rapid solution for fixing torn nylon tents and tarps. I hadn't used the pennies before, and he shared a yarn about camping beneath Alaska's high alpine crags when sudden gusts began pummeling his tent. In less than an hour, one of the corner grommets holding the tarp secure had ripped out, leaving a good portion of the rainfly flapping in the wind.

He reached into his pocket and grabbed a half dozen pennies, found a shot of cord several feet long in his pack, rolled the pennies into a tight bundle, grabbed a fistful of nylon, twisted the tarp, tied off his pennies to form a toggle in the nylon, then made several wraps of the cord around a large rock. Quarters, dimes, nickels, and other coinage works well too, he says.

knot to secure the tablecloth firmly in place atop the picnic table. The other option would be to delegate the four twines, one to each corner. Adjust the tablecloth; pull it taut, and tie the corners to their respective table legs.

DUCT TAPE

I sometimes wonder that if all life on Earth vanished and space explorers came eons later, they wouldn't find remnants of duct tape. Though the tape was originally created to act as a bandage over seams where long sections of sheet metal heating and air-conditioning ducts came together, innovative souls discovered its widespread applicability decades ago. Since then it has been used to patch the fuselage of small airplanes, boats, tents, tarps, clothing, and just about any other item where its tenacious strength and sticky attributes can plug a hole or hold things together until a more permanent fix can be achieved.

Duct tape has evolved far beyond its pragmatic duties of wrapping or patching items, growing to such market popularity that today manufacturers offer it in a wide array of colors and patterns from camouflage to hot pink. There are pageants in which duct tape is the mandatory material for clothing and contests where engineers must make gadgets and other inventions using the magic tape as the main construction material. An increasingly common application has been with airline passengers, who tape elaborate designs on luggage to make it unique among the other baggage plopping onto carousels at their arrival destinations.

In the camping world, it's tops for fixing holes in tent flies or rain gear. With some tent repairs, it helps to first fortify the patch by stitching a rip shut with a needle and dental floss then using crisscross layers of duct tape to add strength and make the area waterproof.

Winding the tape carefully around supportive sticks works wonders to repair broken tent poles or trekking poles; the tape can even be used to create a splint for broken bones. Backcountry hikers and trail runners have long used patches of well-placed duct tape on their heels and toes or along their ankles as preemptive protection against blisters. You can use it to tape a rolled ankle or a sprained wrist. (For comfort, it helps to put napkins or other soft material between the tape and your skin.)

Duct tape comes in a variety of colors. You don't need to pack a whole roll into the woods; just spool off several yards of tape and wind it around a drinking bottle or trekking poles.

Among more creative uses, duct tape becomes the antidote for the stinging spines of buck moth caterpillars in the eastern states. After carefully brushing the caterpillars—also known as Goshen zappers—off your arms or legs with a stick or another object other than your hands, carefully apply a layer of the tape, sticky side down, then lift it away. The caterpillar spines will stick to the tape, safely removing them from your skin.

Duct tape rolled and shaped into a ball, sticky-side out, works well to remove hair, lint, and dirt from sleeping bags and clothing out at camp. Stretch duct tape, sticky-side up, across the ground to form a barrier against insects, mice, and small snakes.

Duct tape also can be rolled the long way to form straps or light-duty rope.

FIRST AID

Knowing what to do when you or another camper has been injured never comes easy when your adrenaline is flowing. And at no time does it flow faster than when one of our immediate family members incurs a sharp cut, broken bone, or life-threatening injury. The "secret" ingredient to maintaining our mental stability—and providing quality assistance to others during an emergency—relies on personal training. In most communities, emergency medical technicians (EMTs) and other professionals offer cardiopulmonary resuscitation (CPR) and first-aid courses ranging from 4 hours to several days.

This is good stuff. For starters, you learn to assess the area surrounding the accident to determine if you, the caregiver, or bystanders are in immediate threat of the same danger afflicting the victim, such as falling rocks, an angry bear, or oncoming vehicle traffic. Most trainers offer an approach to situations that are by nature chaotic and highly uncomfortable; the best trainers will lead you through a methodical process in assessing characteristics of the injury and discerning proper treatment.

Training comes in various levels, from basic CPR and first aid to wilderness EMT courses. When embarking on hiking and camping excursions with others, a preliminary discussion at the trailhead should involve establishing who in the group makes the best medic based upon having the most experience, certifications—and confidence. Sometimes several campers will be well qualified to respond to an array of emergencies. At other times the strongest candidate may possess an outdated certification, but chances are strong that he or she will remember the basics in an emergency. At the end of that trailhead discussion, delegate the most qualified camper to carry the first-aid kit.

At the heart of treating all injuries and other life- or health-threatening emergencies is a suitable first-aid kit. Some campers combine first-aid kits with survival kits, and we'll discuss how to build a combo kit in the pages ahead.

Have you ever wondered why some kits are contained within heavy metal boxes with latching lids while others are much smaller in bulk and packed tightly into small stuff sacks? Like cooking, it's all in the ingredients. For years we carried cumbersome plastic mouthpieces to protect us from fluid-borne pathogens in the event we'd need to perform CPR; nowadays lightweight barriers effect the same function but at a fraction of the bulk and weight. Some kits include elastic compression bandages and several rolls of white surgical tape. Most kits contain one or two pairs of surgical gloves. If you're allergic to latex, look for kits containing nitrile or vinyl alternatives.

A notable discrepancy among manufacturers is the apportionment of gauze bandages they stuff into their kits. Check packing or supplies lists when shopping for kits to become familiar with what's inside. Our preference over the years has been to build custom kits with copious amounts of 3 × 3-inch and 4 × 4-inch gauze bandages; kids run barefoot in summer, and most of our campground first-aid responses have been to purge sand and dirt from wide cuts in the feet, apply multiple gauze patches, and then use direct pressure to stop the bleeding.

Survival and First-Aid Combo Kits

As a creative alternative to packing an over-the-counter first-aid kit, consider making your own and incorporating some survival supplies as well. Surgical tape is a must, but we also carry plenty of duct tape (we don't pack the whole roll) and a roll of electrical tape for other needs in camp. In numerous cases we've used the tougher, more weather-resistant electrical tape or duct tape for holding gauze bandages around cut fingers or over other wounds. Duct tape is readily accessible if you've wound several yards of it tightly around each trekking pole in the preamble to your camping season. We like to wind another several yards of duct tape around our water bottles. As mentioned earlier, the tape comes in handy for fixing torn tent flies and other temporary repairs around camp.

A handy aside to packing along plenty (at least two rolls) of tape is to learn how to tape a rolled ankle. I learned how at a youth basketball court and got

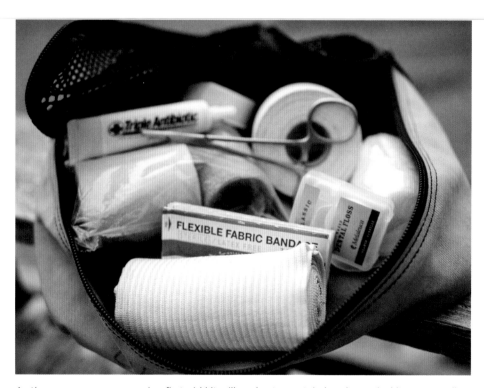

As time goes on, your camping first-aid kit will evolve to contain handy survival items as well.

plenty of practice through the years. For some pre-camping trip fun, watch an online instructional video or two, grab a couple rolls of surgical tape, and practice taping each other up. It's a skill that can turn a potentially unpleasant, truncated trip into one of comfort and completion. Of all the information you'll see, maintaining capillarity (blood circulation) in the toes is critical when beginning the taping process. If you've ever rolled an ankle or broken an arm or leg, you've probably noticed that your caregiver pinches your toes. Though it may seem to have been done to add a comedic element to the situation, it's a test to determine that the whiteness of the pinched flesh returns to normal color within a few heartbeats. That's a sign that the first wraps aren't too tight and haven't compromised circulation.

Additional rolls of prewrap—a thin, foam-based material placed between the skin and the surgical or duct tape to prevent rashes and other discomfort—are well worth the cost and added bulk to your kit. Study the steps in the taping process. Essentially, you're asking patients to hold their toes 90 degrees to their legs (like they are standing on level ground) and then building a set of tape stirrups, a set of figure eights around the rolled ankle, and a series of J-shaped supports beginning on the inside of the leg, just above the ankle and extending up the length of the outside lower leg below the calf.

Magnifying glasses are fun for closer examination of interesting rocks or other small objects as part of recreation, but they morph into a medical instrument when it's time to pluck caterpillar spines, slivers, or other small objects from the skin.

Tweezers are handy to include as you build your custom kit, but a small set of hemostats works wonders for removing stubborn hooks from the mouths of fish or—heaven forbid—stabilizing the end of a hook that's found its way through someone's ear or finger. The immense mechanical advantage of the locking hemostat can be used to crush the barb of the hook, enabling the caregiver to back the hook out of the body.

Thinking of hemostats as precise, high-strength mini pliers will spark many useful ideas in camp. They can tighten small nuts and bolts and hold items in place like a small vise. They can even be used to hold small hooks securely to tie fishing flies.

Dental floss isn't just about hygiene anymore; it lives a double life in many camps, especially if you also pack along some heavy-gauge sewing needles. Repairs to tents, clothing, and other fabric remain durable, and the waxed floss is fairly weather resistant.

A bottle of baby (low-dose) aspirin (nonbuffered) can be a lifesaver should you encounter a camper suffering a heart attack. Of course the person will need special medical attention quickly, but the aspirin can buy precious minutes until the EMTs arrive. Aspirin works as an anticlotting agent by keeping blood platelets from sticking together, preventing clogging of the arteries and helping to keep blood flowing through the heart until medical experts arrive. Many online sources call for a dosage of 325 milligrams, which calculates out to roughly four of the 81 milligram pills that are commonly used as a daily preventative for heart attacks. If you arrive at the scene of a heart attack and have aspirin in your kit, have the victim chew the aspirin and chase it with a swallow of water. Chewing releases the aspirin to the bloodstream faster than swallowing.

 CHARLIE GOES CAMPING

I had climbed about halfway up a 3,700-foot mountain as part of a training run for a grueling race known as the Matanuska Peak Challenge, here in Alaska. The 14-mile course gains an elevation of 9,100 feet and reverses the process for the return route. The race was still three weeks away, and I wanted to pre-run the whole course on a hot, sunny afternoon. But my training took on an abrupt change in focus at around 1,500 feet, when I heard a faint call from the shade of a patch of alders.

I drew closer. A woman in her early 60s asked if I had any baby aspirin.

I did not.

I approached her to find her husband lying near the base of a tree, gasping for breath and in obvious pain.

"It's got to be a heart attack," she said. "But it's hard to believe, as we were hiking at 10,000 feet in the Andes just a couple weeks ago."

She said that she'd already called 911 and that help was on its way. Given the topography and weather conditions in Alaska, however, the time span between an incident, the response, and proper medical attention can mean hours.

A half hour later, a band of hikers approached, one of whom was a nurse. She knelt beside the man, took his pulse, and affirmed that he was indeed suffering from cardiac arrest. He was breathing; his pulse was "steady and thready," she said, and there was no need to begin CPR.

Syringes

These come in various styles and sizes, most with markings delineated in milli-liters (same as cubic centimeters) along their sides. They're handy for their primary duty, administering accurate dosages of medicines, but they turn into your best friends when a fall on the trail or a crash on a mountain bike pushes soil or tiny rock fragments deep into a cut. It's painful, and it's nasty work, but a large pot of warm soapy water and a syringe are by far your best bet to get all the foreign matter out of the cut before you dress the wound. Beyond their medical applications, syringes also blow air and make handy tools for removing particles of fine dust out of the nooks and crannies of cell phones, cameras, or other electronics dropped in the dirt. Get them at pharmaceutical stores.

The weather that day was perfect for hiking and many hikers passed by, but none of them had any aspirin.

Eventually, a helicopter landed on a broad ledge "bench" about 700 feet above us. Another hiker and I raced up the hill to help paramedics pack down a bottle of oxygen, nitroglycerin pills, a litter, and other equipment needed for rescue. The paramedics stabilized the patient with the nitroglycerin but determined that the terrain was too steep to pack him down on the litter. An hour later a huge military chopper hovered overhead. The thrust of its rotors flattened the understory shrubs and denuded the banded forest of its leaves. Dust and debris flew into my eyes and stuck painfully to my contact lenses. The rescue crew managed to keep the chopper flying level near the steep sidehill. Amid the deafening roar of the blades we looked up. A heavy metal basket swayed violently on a steel cable and began descending toward the ground. The paramedics and a couple of us hikers grabbed the basket, lifted the patient into it, and strapped him in tightly for what would probably be the most memorable ride in his life. His wife and I exchanged phone numbers, and I called later that night to discover that he was fully recovered and expected to be released from the hospital in the morning.

The moral of the story is that I now carry small bottles of baby aspirin in the glove compartment of my car, my daypacks, even my pockets. Pack soft cloth or a gauze bandage inside to keep the tiny pills from rattling against one another and the sides of the bottle so they don't turn into powder as you bounce along on your hikes, runs, or other strenuous activity.

Snakebite Treatment

You might have seen old-timey Western movies where the hero gets bitten by a venomous snake (before he even gets into the gunfight at high noon!), cuts two distinct *X*-shaped slices across the puncture made by each of the fangs, then vigorously sucks the venom out with his mouth. Though times have changed and modern technology has given us snakebite kits that include vacuum pumps to perform the functions described above, treating snakebites is not that simple. For starters, snakes' fangs are curved, which means the exact place where they've injected their venom is not directly below the position of the wound. Also, although about 20 percent of snakebites are "dry bites," meaning they contain no venom, when venom *is* injected it enters the bloodstream too quickly to be extracted by suction.

Proper snakebite treatment in the field includes first moving the victim and other campers away from the snake and then getting an accurate description of the snake to help health care providers determine the likely species and administer the appropriate antivenin, which counteracts the effects of the venom on the body's muscular and neurological systems. Do not ice the wound, add heat, or add a compress. Unlike nosebleeds or other open wounds, position the afflicted appendage—most likely the lower leg—at or below the level of the heart. Remove watches, bracelets, or other jewelry that might cut into the skin in the advent of swelling. If you are in the backcountry and not able to summon emergency medical services, begin the trek toward a place where you can get help. Move slowly, and have the victim walk without a pack or anything else that would increase the level of exertion.

Splints

In desert areas where small woody cane or other stiff plant material is not available, try packing along one of the lighter versions of an air splint. For feet and ankles, these splints are composed of lightweight plastic stirrups with an inflatable cuff to add support. Popsicle sticks (or anything rigid and approximating those dimensions) make satisfactory finger splints.

For broken legs and arms, trekking poles will prove themselves invaluable for stabilization. Elevate the arm or leg slightly above the ground, place the poles gently alongside the break, then lace the splint together with your tape. If you are without trekking poles but someone in the group has a daypack or backpack with an internal frame, open the top flap and look inside for conspicuous Velcro flaps. Inside these long internal pockets you'll often find the "pack stays," flat straps of aluminum, magnesium, or carbon fiber. These provide rigidity to the pack for the hiker, but become makeshift splint material when you need to fabricate a splint.

Hydrogen Peroxide

Open wounds need attention quickly to prevent infection. Rubbing alcohol and hydrogen peroxide are two favored washes when it comes to cleansing wounds, but campers rarely pack these two weighty items. A great alternative if someone in your group wears contact lenses might be the saline solution used for cleaning or storing those lenses. Even better, some lens cleaning systems use hydrogen peroxide for protein removal. The hydrogen peroxide sold for dressing wounds and the peroxide-based lens cleaning kits both contain 3 percent hydrogen peroxide.

Bandages

Based upon our camping experiences, gauze is the one medical supply you hope you never need—but when you do need it, you'll want a lot of it. Much of what gauze does best in a serious injury lies in applying direct pressure to the wound. The gauze acts as an absorbent pad to soak up the blood. When it becomes saturated with blood, you leave it right there and add another layer, and on and on. For small injuries you can usually get by with a single or double layer. Long scrapes from running or falling off a mountain bike will have you appreciating the 4 × 4-inch versions, while the 3 × 3-inch versions lend themselves better to little scrapes, scratches, and cuts from glass. Though gauze is often available in smaller dimensions, I stay with the larger sizes, which can be folded in half to amply cover smaller wounds.

In a pinch, picnic napkins, feminine napkins, paper towels, toilet paper, or even sleeves cut from a clean shirt or other clothing can help stop bleeding.

Barriers, Shields, and Other Resuscitating Devices

Cardiopulmonary resuscitation (CPR) demands training, and even with proper certification and practice, clearing the airway for respiration gets tricky, especially when the victim is lying on uneven ground. Lightweight plastic breathing tubes with a protective membrane and safety valves that contain fluids from the victim sell for less than $20 at medical supply stores. You still have to know how to thrust the chin and tilt the head to clear the airway properly, but the breathing devices take care of the rest.

Epinephrine

Epinephrine and its delivery device, the EpiPen, could prevent you or a camping neighbor from going into anaphylactic shock from bee or wasp stings. Learning how to use one of these pens has never been easier; manufacturers have devised a simple, spring-loaded mechanism to drive in the needle and deliver the epinephrine. In addition, suppliers include detailed instructions that will lead you through the steps of disarming the safety latch and handy diagrams to show you where to place the pen on top of the quadriceps (the largest muscle in the upper leg).

Include one in your kit even if nobody in your immediate family is allergic to stings, as your kids will probably want to invite friends or begin chumming with newfound friends on family outings. Summer coincides with the building of large wasp colonies, and folks who've never been stung have no idea if they are allergic or not. You can caution your kids and their friends to stay clear of the giant nests hanging from limbs of trees, but they'll want to explore, and wasps can emerge from underground nests near paths in the forest. Epinephrine is useless once it has been frozen and thus must be removed from your kit when repacking for any winter camping trips. EpiPens also have expiration dates.

Diphenhydramine

Most commonly known by the brand name Benadryl, diphenhydramine, an antihistamine, comes in handy should somebody camping with or near you react to eating shellfish, have an allergic reactions to pollen, or suffer from a variety of other conditions that cause the body to produce histamine. Benadryl has been used to treat everything from sleep disorders to hay fever and itching, sneezing, and watery eyes caused by colds, and is often administered as a precursor to the EpiPen in situations involving bee stings or other reactions that produce hives on the skin or a tightening in the throat.

Pollen Index

While it's a good idea to pack along Benadryl or another over-the-counter treatment for hay fever and other allergies, many online sources offer local or regional pollen indexes. These handy tools not only tell you what plant, shrub, or tree species are generating pollen at a specific time of the year but also give you forecasts that predict blooms for up to a week ahead. Though seasoned campers usually have a handle on a specific pollen that affects them, newcomers to the camping experience might not have been exposed to various types of pollen in the high concentrations found in the woods. In the northern states, trees generate the predominant pollen as the camping season gets under way in early summer. Then the grasses kick in. In southern-tier states such as Texas, grass pollen, mold, and tree pollen counts kick in earlier.

Rainfall and wind are key factors in pollen generation. Rain in early spring jump-starts plants into their life cycles, which brings on the pollen; rain after pollen begins falling or blowing in the wind drives it to the ground. Light and steady rain works best for keeping pollen out of the air, but heavy downpours can knock grass pollens to the ground and break them into smaller particles, which then come back to haunt folks with allergies even worse when the ground dries out and the wind begins to blow.

HYGIENE

Though you might make an overnight camping trip without amenities such as shampoo and conditioner, toothbrush and toothpaste, floss, lotions, deodorant, and other toiletries, you can assemble a camp-ready kit that's always ready to go for multiple days in the woods. Look for travel-size tubes of toothpaste, contact lens cleaning solution, lotions, shampoo, and other hygiene needs at your local grocery or department store. For ease in camping, look for product lines that combine shampoo and conditioner together in the same container.

When it comes to the containers themselves, look for ones with screw-on tops rather than flip tops, which can open inadvertently during your travels and leave your shower kit a swamp of sticky goo.

You often leave trips to the dentist with complimentary toothbrushes, toothpaste, and floss. These make great additions to your camp shower kit. Though hotel-size bars of soap offer convenience in size, they're difficult to store in your kit after their initial use. Small sandwich bags keep these little soaps contained and prevent them from sliming up other contents in your kit, but they eventually turn into a glob and fill the grooves of the resealable bag, making them hard to contain. Body wash, on the other hand, comes in small bottles or tubes with screw-on tops and is easy to store when you're done.

Bathroom towels like those used at home are typically larger than what you need at camp. Beach towels are a good size for lying on grass or sand at the beach and can double as a bathing towel at the camp shower, sauna, or public bathhouse. Towels that measure about half between a standard bathroom towel and a hand towel (about 18 × 24 inches and offered in many hotels) are perfect for wiping moisture away from your body. They dry quickly in an afternoon breeze and don't take up nearly as much space, especially when packing for large families or groups.

Changes in weather are sure to occur as long as the Earth keeps spinning and mixing up zones of air warmed by the sun.

CHAPTER 13

WEATHER-WISE

AFTER A DAY OF FISHING, berry picking, and swimming under the hot sun, evening had arrived—and with it a bank of clouds that thickened with each passing hour and brought darkness much sooner than on the other days we'd camped. By the time we'd all crawled into the tent, its walls flexed with the hint of a breeze, and the stand of tall Norway pines towering 50 feet over our heads begin to murmur as the wind hit their tops. Darkness always seems to magnify sensitivity among campers. We'd all crawled into our respective sleeping bags, but none of us slept as the pines began to roar and dead branches from high above snapped off and landed near the tent with a resounding thud.

That was all it took for my dad to unzip from his bag and tell us to muster out by the car. With dim flashlights we headed past the picnic table and assembled near the family station wagon. The woods that we'd appreciated for its serene setting and shade from the sun just hours before now threatened to throw down giant trees and crush us. A major portion of this particular campground had been closed two years before, after a tornado touched down and left the huge pines snapped at their trunks and strewn about like jackstraws.

By the time Dad had zipped the tent shut and met us at the car, we had panicked.

"Where are the keys?" he shouted to Mom above the din.

"The keys?" she responded. "I thought you had them."

My younger brother, Matt, who had usually been so quiet as a kid, suddenly shrieked.

"The keys!"

Dad fumbled through his pockets and eventually found them. He started the car, turned on the headlights, and we began navigating our way among branches on the road. As an air traffic controller, Dad had briefed thousands of pilots on the weather at the airport, and now he drew upon his meteorological experience to guide us out of the path of a severe low-pressure system with the potential of building into a tornado. Not only did he discern which way the system was moving, but he knew a narrow logging road that would lead us out of the tall pines and to a series of low willow swamps, where we waited out the squall.

HOW WEATHER WORKS

Without overly geeking out about its scientific details, weather, as we know it, results from the heat of the sun and the Earth's rotation against its own atmosphere. We often say that the sun rises in the east, and though that's acceptable, the reality is that the Earth spins counterclockwise on its axis so that its surface races from the west toward the sun at approximately 1,000 miles per hour at the equator. That much speed creates a significant stirring of the air, which maintains the northeast trade winds of the Northern Hemisphere. At the same time, the radiant power of the sun creates an upwelling of hot air at the equator. It rises and travels north to the mid latitudes, where it gets into an argument with winds that predominantly flow west. There, at about 30 degrees north latitude—and smack in middle of the United States—air from the equator skirmishes with the cooler air of the north, and the party begins.

What does all this mean to family campers?

Weather never rests. The Earth spins, creating countervailing winds through the latitudes, and high and low pressure systems develop in proximity to each other in a halfhearted attempt to bring the atmosphere into equilibrium—a fleeting rarity, which means that you, as campers, will want to build a "weather eye" like my dad did, assimilating the knowledge necessary to get you and yours out of a meteorological jam that could ruin your trip.

Fronts

Fronts refer to the edges of a body of air that encroaches upon another body of air when the temperature between the two differs widely. A cold front refers

Self-destructing sunshine: Hot sun hits the wetlands between mountain ranges and sucks the moisture from lakes, streams, or other waterways upward most of the day. In late afternoon, the cloud tops have risen to heights where the cool air of the upper atmosphere pushes the clouds to their saturation point, and we wind up with heavy showers for about an hour.

to cold air driving itself like a wedge under warmer air. Cold air sinks, and warm air rises, so you'd think the two would get along; but air masses are sometimes like two siblings in the back seat. As the warmer air makes room for the cold, it rises along the leading edge of the cold front, where it often makes a fuss, forming clouds that produce lightning and thunder, severe thundershowers, and hail. While rapid formation of isolated, towering cumulous clouds indicates a cold front, the arrival of a warm front usually comes with high stratus, making the entire sky overcast with clouds that can mean a drizzle for the next couple of days. A difference of 20 degrees between the two air masses can cause significant weather developments during your campout.

When cold fronts out of Canada assert themselves against the warm, moist air traveling northward from the Gulf of Mexico, vast regions of the southern and central United States see thunderstorms and rain. But the process can turn violent. Often in spring and fall, masses of warm air linger too long and don't rise

The evening moon rising above wisps of broken cirrostratus portends great weather in the morning.

in time to climb beyond the encroaching cold front. When warm air masses get caught under the creeping cold fronts, they race along, looking for a way out. In their panic they often create wind shears, meaning that winds accelerate in opposing directions at different altitudes under the front. When the axis of the wind shears grows unstable, they flip from a horizontal flow to a vertical flow, tighten up, and a tornado is born.

More than 1,000 tornadoes form in the United States each year—far more than anywhere else in the world. The formation of these funnels in the Texas panhandle, Oklahoma, Nebraska, South Dakota, and eastern Colorado have earned the region the moniker "Tornado Alley." Tornadoes can form suddenly and travel at an average speed of 30 miles per hour.

High- and Low-Pressure Systems

As the Earth twirls in its yearly pirouette around the sun, the heating of the winds near the equator and cooling of the winds near the poles creates blobs of air with mixed temperatures. Differing air temperatures equate to different atmospheric pressure. Generally, low-pressure systems dominate the polar easterlies in the high Arctic and create corresponding high-pressure systems in the lower latitudes (United States) in which most of us camp. But it's not that simple. Air of differing temperatures carries different weights—at any latitude. Cold air is denser than warm air and wants to fall to the Earth's surface. Warm air is less dense and wants to climb. How do we distinguish relative differences between the two? The answer goes back to seventeenth-century physicists, who proposed that the weight of the air could be measured with a device called a barometer, and that the weight would change as the instrument was moved in and out of high- or low-pressure areas.

Of interest to us campers, however, is that these high- and low-pressure centers determine the direction and velocity of wind. Low-pressure areas twirl upward and create counterclockwise air movement on the ground. High-pressure areas, on the other hand, push down and create winds that flow clockwise around their centers. That means you can stand with your back to the wind and determine that lower pressures are on your left and higher pressures are on your right. As the hours progress, you might detect that the wind direction has changed, which would indicate movement of the two systems.

Mares' tails, thin wisps of high cirrus clouds, indicate moisture collecting in the air—and that rain may be on its way.

Back to the beauty of barometers: Weather stations at various locales in the region where you're camping report their respective barometric pressures every hour. National weather forecasters then incorporate the measurements of barometric pressures from the sites into a computer generated graphic, and like a dot-to-dot map, the data forms lines—like the growth rings in a tree—of stations with similar pressures. The closer these concentric lines of differing pressure are together, the more wind you can expect. Intense low-pressure areas that get pinned under an advancing cold front commonly produce tornado conditions. The proximity of the highs and lows to each other also plays a role in what you can expect for wind and precipitation conditions.

CLOUDS AS PREDICTORS

As family campers, it's fun to develop sources of weather information you can trust. Weather forecasters have made great strides in the accuracy of their predictions, and a plethora of phone apps can keep you up to date, but nothing matches your own eyes and wits when it comes to predicting weather during your campout.

My dad instilled within us kid campers a love and a knowledge of clouds as indicators of weather. Basically there are three types of clouds: stratus, cumulous, and cirrus. And all three have overlapping characteristics.

As a rule, cirrus clouds are high (30,000 feet or higher) and composed of ice crystals in the upper atmosphere. The sun and the moon are usually visible through these clouds, and they portend fair weather. Examples of these clouds include "mares' tails," wispy white splotches that punctuate a blue sky. Mares' tails usually signify the arrival of a cold front, and if the sky remains clear, it's safe to assume that the cold front has pushed off the warm front and you're headed for more of the same fair weather.

Stratus clouds, on the other hand, tend to lie at lower altitudes and cover the whole sky. These are typically laden with moisture. You cannot see the sun or moon through them, and if it's not raining now, it will be within hours. A reliable predictor of precipitation in the hours or days ahead is when stratus rides high in the sky to form cirrostratus. A telltale sign of cirrostratus, and an accompanying warm front with its precipitation, is often a ring around the moon at night.

Cumulus clouds are puffy and sometimes ominous. These clouds can originate at various altitudes and are commonly a source of entertainment and subjects of pictures for shapes that resemble faces, angels, animals, and other objects. Well-isolated cumulus clouds wafting across the sky at higher altitudes often mean continued fair weather; however, these clouds can signify changing

Puffy white cumulous clouds, well isolated and wafting across the sky during the day, often mean settled weather.

weather, especially if their bases are at a low altitude and they build vertically to gargantuan heights over the course of several hours. In this condition, the cumulous clouds are heavy with moisture picked up from lakes, rivers, or cool ground. The moisture rises toward the cooler air of the upper atmosphere, where it condenses, forms raindrops, and falls downward within the cloud. In many cases the moisture breaks free of the cloud and falls to earth as heavy rain. But these tall clouds sometimes have a mind of their own and won't let raindrops fall. Powerful upwelling energy overcomes gravity and sucks the raindrops all the way back to the top of the cloud, where they add a layer of ice. This cycle may repeat itself several times and turn tiny raindrops into hail the size of a golf ball—or larger—before gravity overcomes the upwelling cycle of the cloud and the hail falls to defoliate trees and put dents in cars.

Of all the cloud forms, rapidly building cumulous clouds indicate the most drastic change in weather. The air is often left cool and fresh after a hailstorm, but in the meantime you'll want to find ample cover to protect you and yours from the falling white projectiles.

Forgot your barbecue tongs? Split a couple of thin slices off a block of firewood and you've got the tools to keep the hot dogs—and the good times—rolling.

CHAPTER 14

SUBSTITUTE THIS FOR THAT

IT'S NOT THAT YOU didn't make a list and go through it back at home, checking off important items here and there. But you've arrived at your campsite after hours of driving, set up the tent—and discovered that you forgot the air mattresses. Never fear. Make this chapter your go-to for hacks to get out of a camping jam with substitute solutions and a way of thinking that can turn lemons into a lemon meringue pie.

For example, when is a wooden match not a wooden match?

When the end is sharpened and used to clean your teeth in place of forgotten toothpaste, toothbrush, and floss.

On our very first family campout, my dad forgot the camp stove, which meant everything from eggs and toast to pancakes to beans, potatoes, and hamburgers would have to be cooked over an open fire. Not only did we survive, but we came to relish the smoky taste of burgers and the challenge of finding dry driftwood at the nearby lake to burn. It took our camping experience to a whole new dimension.

FORGOTTEN AIR MATTRESSES, COTS, AND SLEEPING BAGS

So you've forgotten your air mattress. If you remembered a cot, you're in fine shape and can make do with your extra clothing arranged under your sleeping bag to add a bit of padding. Perhaps you packed personal flotation devices (lifejackets) in anticipation of canoe trips out on the lake. Bingo! You've found the perfect pillow. As you attempt to solve problems associated with items missing from your camping gear, it helps to think of those items in a hierarchy of function. In other words, what they do. For many, the primary duty of an air mattress is to provide a buffer between the hips or the spine and the hard ground. Delegating extra shirts, windbreakers, beach towels, or bathing suits as makeshift padding under the more sensitive areas of the body can make nights bearable. Depending on the locale and the season in which you are camping, you might find loose leaves or other soft material to stuff under the floor of the tent. Placing dried grass clippings under the floor for padding sometimes works, as does moving the tent to the soft sand of a beach.

As for a forgotten cot, canoe paddles arranged with a PFD and extra clothing spread out on top can keep the shoulder blades and back aligned and provide an extra margin of comfort through the night. Experiment with arranging the paddles with their broad ends side by side or opposing, with the paddle and yoke spread about 18 inches apart. Collapsed lawn or picnic chairs can provide a flat framework under critical areas of the spine. The secret to a comfortable sleeping system lies in the padding you can find to put between you and the ground. Think of any extra tarps, boat covers, tablecloths, bags, or sacks you may have brought with you. Among other creative avenues to consider, pull the headrests from the seats of your car and arrange them in a comfortable array. Or sleep in the car with the seats reclined.

FORGOTTEN COOKING UTENSILS

You arrive at camp, start unpacking the vehicle, and realize that a large box containing pots, pans, dishes, bowls, cups, and other utensils has been left behind. When is firewood not firewood? When it's been split into flat strips to form dinner plates, whittled thin to form chopsticks, or carved to form spoons, forks, and even ladles. That can of peaches you were saving for dessert? Open it and enjoy. Save the can—and the lid—for cooking innovation in the days to come. Hamburger that you molded into uniform

Forgot your taco shells? Try throwing the meat, cheese, and other ingredients into a small bag of chips to make a taco salad instead.

patties at home can be recombined to make meat loaf inside the can. That same empty can will be your coffeepot come morning, after you place it near the coals of the campfire. Paper towels, napkins, or fine-meshed clothing material (shirtsleeves) placed over the top of the can and pushed down in the middle to form a funnel will work just fine as your coffee filter. Sure, you can always backtrack to the nearest town and procure the stuff you're missing, but if adventure tops your list of cravings, you're off to a good start.

RAIN GEAR, FORGOTTEN (OR PURPOSELY LEFT BEHIND)

Rain gear ranks among the most common of items left behind, and not always by way of forgetting. Clear skies and an optimistic forecast for more of the same on the day you depart for a weekend of bliss may turn out to be the classic setup for foul weather to set in, but it can also be the catalyst for creativity with trash bags. If you've ever hung out with someone who sews or watched them cut out a pattern for a dress or other garment, this is your big chance to try your hand with scissors or a sharp knife as you cut a shallow half-moon out of the closed end of the bag, right at the center. Next, cut two more holes for the arms, one to each side of the neck opening. Sure, they look corny, but in a popular campground, chances are good that you won't be alone. Thin tarps and space blankets make wonderful substitutes for forgotten rain gear, but don't cut holes in them—you'll need them at full strength under your sleeping bag and to keep other goods dry if the wet weather holds out. Just wear them about the shoulders like a cape. Unlike trash bags, most standard-size space blankets will offer ample coverage well below the knees.

TOWELS

Towels can be forgotten altogether if they are packed in the same duffel bag or container, but if a single towel has been forgotten by a family member or friend, the simple fix is to assess who has the largest towel in the group and then tear it in half. But towels—at least good ones—are tough, and you'll need a sharp knife to nick the edging at the halfway point to get the process on its way. You can also cut the entire width of the towel with the knife.

If the entire lot of campers has forgotten their towels, the other standby involves using your cleanest dirty clothing to dry off after swimming or showering. Invariably, one piece of clothing always seems to escape the mud, dust, and body odor better than others, and that will be your towel for the trip. While cotton isn't the material of choice when you need wick-away qualities for evaporating sweat and conserving body heat, most T-shirts are made of cotton, which makes them excellent makeshift towels. One trick to bathing without a towel is to take a dirty T-shirt to a lake or stream where you can rinse it out and wring it dry several times then hang it in the sun to dry.

If you've forgotten towels, you've probably forgotten soap, conditioner, and shampoo. Swimming in lakes or relaxing in streams during the heat of the day often accomplishes the task of cleanliness and leaves campers feeling fresh.

TENT

While it would seem obvious not to forget the obvious when packing items before embarking on a trip, we sometimes drive away from home leaving the most essential piece of our camping equipment "in a good place, where we won't forget it." If you're a family or a group of friends crowded into a car, the weather turns rainy, and you've forgotten the tent, you'll be seeing one another up close and personal for the next few nights as you take turns reclining in the seats and learning new skills in how to get sufficient sleep while sitting up.

 CHARLIE GOES CAMPING

Showers were a must for me every day when I lived in a tent during my first hot summer as a logger in Minnesota's north woods. Then again, there was the laundry. Each day I'd return from the woods, my shirts and pants wet with sweat and sap from the trees. I'd met an old woodsman earlier that summer who shared a trick that afforded such efficiency that I sometimes wonder why don't employ it here at home. The process was simple and involved only two sets of clothes: I'd step out of my boots, enter the shower stall fully dressed, pour a small mound of laundry soap on each shoulder, turn on the hot water, and work my clothes into a huge lather with my hands. At the same time I worked the dirt out of my clothing, I massaged away the aches and pains from a long day running the chainsaw and swinging axes. When my clothing smelled clean and the soap had been rinsed away, I'd strip down and hit my hair and body with a generous dose of dish soap, which seemed to take the pine pitch out of my hair better than most shampoo. I'd emerge from the shower, change into dry clothes, walk to my tent camp, and hang my laundry on the clothesline to dry so that I could swap out my clothes and repeat the cycle the next day.

This isn't the end of the world (think international flights). If you've packed along tarps, hammocks, pads, sleeping bags, and the other stuff, you're in better shape than you might think. For example, large coniferous trees can accommodate small groups of campers near their stumps.

Depending on the configuration of your vehicle, there are a few tricks you can try. Years ago we'd make sure to take the keys out of the ignition and then crawl under our pickups, and that's still an option to owners of some trucks. The evolution of hatchbacks, crossovers, and SUVs offers the possibility of stretching out by extending your feet and legs under the rear bumper of the vehicle and leaving the hatch open. A couple caveats, though: Turn off your dome light, and use a stick or trekking pole to ensure that the lid stays in its upright position in case a breeze springs up.

As a measure of safety, especially if your camping experience involves alcohol or recreational drugs, designate the folks sleeping outside the vehicle as keepers of the keys. This should ensure that nobody winds up driving over anybody else and reduce the likelihood of someone starting the engine, producing carbon monoxide that could asphyxiate the folks sleeping inside. Having two folks sleep under the hatch allows two more campers to put the seats into full reclining positions for total accommodation of four.

In some campgrounds you may find that pavilions are fair game, depending on the season, campground rules, and the locale. Then again, you might hit a stretch of dry weather and enjoy sleeping under the stars.

Knowing a blueberry hot spot adds a lot of fun and flavor to late-summer camping trips.

CHAPTER 15

EAT THIS, NOT THAT

SOMETIMES IT'S HARD to imagine that everything going into our bodies in terms of nourishment ultimately comes from the land. Transportation, packaging, and agriculture have gone a long way toward providing convenient meals in our everyday lives at home.

It doesn't have to be that way at camp.

Wild foraging, fishing, and gathering as part of the camping experience adds a fresh perspective on our place in the food chain, demonstrates our dependence on the environment, and the calls upon our stewardship to take care of it. A welcome side effect of the wild foraging mentality is the hours of fun it provides, and families may wind up making it the focus of their trips.

A bit of ecological knowledge and an eye for plant identification lie at the heart of eating wild. Proper identification of plants, berries, nuts, and other potential wild foods should be paramount among wild harvesters, as various edible species of mushrooms and berries have poisonous look-alikes. Do not subscribe to the myth that if birds or animals can eat a particular berry or mushroom, we can eat it too. Their digestive systems have evolved to safely process foods that would put us on our deathbed.

Countless guides and online blogs will clue you in to regional and seasonal wild foraging events that will put good eats in your bowl or on your plate. Interpretive displays near some camping areas offer detailed explanations about what's edible and what's not.

Seasonality plays a huge role in what's out there for the picking and eating. In early summer, for example, few berry-producing species will offer anything to harvest. A telltale sign that you're too early is when you find blossoms instead of fruit. In many of the northern-tier states, that all changes in June and July, when berry-producing plants and shrubs ripen up and bear their plump blueberries, strawberries, and other delicious orbs.

MUSHROOMS

Springtime in many forested regions also means that wild mushroom season is under way. Proper identification of mushrooms is key in determining poisonous from edible species. Gather the mushrooms, slice them, and add them to your salads or use them to top a tasty grilled steak. Bountiful harvesting may warrant preserving some mushrooms to enjoy back at home. (**Warning:** Gathering and eating wild mushrooms is not advised unless there is a true expert in your party.)

Some mushrooms look pretty, like this fly agaric in Alaska, but they can be deadly. Know your species before you pick them for food.

WILD GREENS

Another wild treasure worth looking for just after the snow melts in spring will be the emergent ferns, nettles, and other wild salad ingredients. Though many species of ferns grow bitter and tough within weeks of emerging in spring, look for them early on, when they have risen just a few inches above the dead leaves from the previous autumn. Chances are good that you'll find them tender and succulent. Pick those with tops that are tightly curled. Scrape off any brown skin-like covering and enjoy, raw or cooked.

Campers with access to beaches can walk in the gravel above the high-tide line and look for tender greens such as lovage, which makes salads pop and adds a cilantro-like flavor to grilled or baked fish fillets. Lovage is known by different names regionally, and tastes best when it's harvested at a height of less than 6 inches. If it's bountiful, tie the stems into tight bunches with floss or light twine, hang them upside down, and dry for use throughout the year.

Learn your ferns. The stems of fiddleheads that are taller than sprouts contain toxic spores. Don't dine on ferns that have risen to such heights as the one pictured here.

SPRUCE TIPS

When late May and early June come to Alaska, spruce trees put forth a new growth at the end of each needled twig. The new tips are lighter green than the rest of the needles, and the delineation in color between the light and the dark is where you want to cut them off.

Spruce tips harvested on early-spring camping trips make sweet and tasty jellies and syrups for topping toast and pancakes.

BERRIES

Among berries to harvest in the wild, look for strawberries in mid- to late June. They prefer sandy, well-drained areas in grassy openings near the edges of the woods, where they can get plenty of sun. Wild raspberries follow a similar time line in the scheme of ripening; they prefer semi-open areas and grow in tight clusters of woody canes.

Search inside forested areas supporting pine trees for blueberries in July and August. Pines trees are often indicators of the acidic soils in which blueberry bushes thrive.

Watermelon berries, as they're known in Alaska, and twisted stalk elsewhere along their range on the West Coast, not only taste like watermelon but also provide great hydration.

FISHING

Fishing constitutes one of oldest methods of capturing a meal. Besides the suspense and excitement that comes from the activity, the whole family can enjoy fresh protein during the camping trip. Most if not all states have detailed fishing regulations as to where, when, and what tackle you can use on various species. Like plant identification, knowing your fish will not only keep you out of trouble with the local fishery authorities for harvesting protected species or species not in season, but the knowledge will pay off in learning key habitats, feeding habits, and how and when to fish for the best success.

Across the southern states, look for bass, crappies, catfish, bluegills, and bream in lakes and streams. These fish frequent shallow ponds and will often take artificial lures that flash, like spinners or spoons, but they will also bite baits looking like large worms or other food. Regulations in some states allow live bait, such as worms or minnows; others permit only artificial lures.

Many of these same species live in the waters of central and northern states, but where waters are deeper in these regions, additional species to catch include northern pike, trout, walleye, and perch.

Depending on the bottom structure (think underwater topography) of the lake, some of the best fishing opportunities lurk near shore. Drop-offs near a beach are a good bet, and streams flowing in and out of reservoirs or lakes also hold an attraction for higher concentrations of fish.

As for fishing gear, when it comes to foraging, the racks at sporting goods stores are lined with hundreds of options. If fishing as foraging means less technology to you, try the basic hook, line, sinker, and long stick approach. For this fun method of fishing, pack along a spool with at least 50 feet of light but strong braided nylon fishing line. Add to that 30 feet of light monofilament (12-pound test) and an assortment of hooks. You can either buy or tie your own flies. In campgrounds where it is allowed (check local, state, and federal laws on cutting small trees), look for slender willows or other small trees that are straight and stand 5 to 8 feet high. (In a pinch, you can use the same sticks for roasting marshmallows.) Cut one of those and refine it to a fishing pole by removing small branches and twigs. To rig the line, start with an end of the braided nylon line and tie a clove hitch with an overhand backing knot at the base of the pole. Run the braided line parallel to the pole and tie another clove

Homemade fishing poles made from sticks and line offer a link back to the primitive practice of harvesting protein.

hitch and backing knot at the tip. Rigging the pole this way ensures that you won't lose a big fish if it snaps the tip off your pole.

As for the length of the braided nylon fishing line that goes into the water, it also should approximate the length of the pole. Cut it off and tie a double figure-eight loop at its end. Cut off about 3 feet of monofilament line and tie a double figure-eight loop in one end. Stick the loop end of the monofilament partially through the loop in the braided nylon, then feed the end of the monofilament through the monofilament loop and pull it down so that the two lines lock neatly together. Tie a hook or a fly on the other end. You're ready to fish. Casting your homemade rig involves a swinging motion to get your lure as far offshore as possible. This rig works great in lakes, rivers, and small streams.

The alternative method, if a stick is not available, is to make a throwing line. This fun way of fishing involves unwinding the braided nylon line, monofilament leader, and hook from a short stick; laying the line in neat loops on the ground; then tossing the baited hook far out into the water. An imperative piece to achieving distance with your fishing rig lies with weight placed about a foot above the hook. Look for small stones with shapes that allow you to harness them with a clove hitch. (See the "Knots to Know" chapter in this book.) Rocks shaped slightly like hourglasses work best so that the line doesn't slip off. For another version of the rig, carve a wooden float or bobber as an option in the throwing-line setup. The wooden float will need enough buoyancy to support the hook line and stone sinker. Rigging this way allows you to suspend the bait off the bottom of the lake. Incorporating a float also adds weight to the end of the line, which adds distance to your cast when you throw it; in some fishing situations you might want to forgo tying on a rock sinker altogether.

Three ways to store the homemade rigs include winding the line lengthwise on a footlong board, winding the line around the circumference of a narrow stick, or stuffing the line into a repurposed yogurt or plastic storage container, which keeps it ready to cast at a moment's notice. The secret to the container is to punch a small hole in the bottom and then tie a knot large enough that the end of the line won't slide through. Having the end of the line secured to the container ensures that you won't cast your entire rig out to sea. Stack the line randomly within the container, hang the hook on the rim at an angle that hides the barb, then snap on the lid.

CLAMS

Many coastal states offer opportunities to dig clams. The trick to successful clam digging is to plan your trip in sync with the month's lowest tides. Local convenience stores carry (they mostly give them away) small pamphlets known as tide tables; there are also phone apps that will let you know when the tide is out. The folks working at local shops can also fill you in on public access points to clamming areas and provide other valuable knowledge. In many states, management of clams as a natural resource falls under the state fisheries department, and harvest limits per digger, per day show up in the fishing regulations.

For clamming you'll want a bucket or other suitable container for carrying the clams, rubber boots, light gloves, and a shovel, known in many parts of the world as a tiling spade. The tiling spade has a long, slender nose in comparison to standard shovel shapes and will allow you to get down through the sand with more ease. When it comes to locating clams, watch for tiny spurts of water coming from the sand as you walk along. Other telltale signs include suspicious dimples in the sand. Try to push the shovel into the sand about 4 inches away from the dimple instead of directly over it so that you don't smash the clam. The digging skills will come naturally within just a few minutes, and you'll be on your way to some delicious chowder and other meals.

When the diggin's done, your clamming experience isn't yet over; you'll still have to clean the clams. Some clammers prefer to let the clams take in freshwater laced with cornmeal in the theory that it cleans out their innards. For eating in camp, bring a pot of salt water to a boil, toss in the clams, and let them cook until the shells open wide. Remove the clams, shuck the meat, dip in butter, and enjoy.

For home preservation, some folks use the cornmeal washing method for a couple of hours before cleaning their catch; others just grab a knife and start shucking shells. Some species of clams lend themselves to removing the stomachs and eating only the necks; others taste great eaten whole. Clams for eating at home should be frozen after they are shucked then cooked thoroughly in a kettle of boiling salt water.

FROGS

Frog legs make for tasty eats if you're camping near wetlands, particularly in the southeast states. Most frog "giggers" prefer to go out at night when the frogs are plentiful and easier to harvest with lights. As a precaution, watch out for venomous snakes, which often haunt the same areas where you'll be catching frogs.

After you've been lucky, take the point of a small, sharp knife and remove the skin and feet from the legs. The meat will resemble the texture and color of a chicken drumstick. Season the legs and throw them in a pan with melted butter; or season them, roll them in flour, then dip them in a milk-and-egg mix and then a bowl of crushed crackers or dry breakfast cereal before tossing them into hot oil for a deep-fried taste.

Camping demands the use of all five senses, and when you add social stimulation with large groups, it can trip the overload switch on littles. If you think of it ahead of time, it's often best to pull your toddler out of the mix and into the quiet, where you can ground the little one in comfort and intimacy.

CHAPTER 16

WHEN KIDS REVOLT

CAMPING CAN HAVE a lot of unpredictable moments, but perhaps some of the worst can be when your kids melt down from heat, hunger, boredom, lack of sleep—or combinations thereof.

Let's face it: Family camping means the experience is the sum of its parts. And those parts are the individuals in the group. A 2-year-old constrained for long hours in a car seat on a bucket-list camping trip across the southern states carries disproportionate weight in the collective direction you're moving when she goes into an inconsolable screaming fit in the middle of an interstate highway. You may find yourself pushing her in a stroller around the parking lot of a windblown truck stop in Arizona. Don't look at your watch. You've nowhere else to be but right here. With this child. In this moment. Take a deep breath. Look around.

You're camping.

In camping as with other rewarding family activities, the secret is the ability to adapt. Nature provides no shortage of challenges and rewards, to which any seasoned camper will attest, but add the mix of different personalities and you've compounded the list of variables when it comes to expectations for the trip. For starters, nearly everyone piling into the car has preconceptions of what he or she hopes the camping experience holds in store. Teenage boy wants to meet teenage girl—and vice versa. The 5-year-old wants to catch fish or frogs. You, the caregivers or parents, want respite from the constraints of your jobs, scheduled appointments, and other components of the daily grind. The 2-year-old screaming in the back seat? Who knows?

But you're here. And we've been here. And we'll go here in the years ahead.

Most meltdowns among kids have more to do with traveling to the camping area than in the activities of the camping area itself. With a little thinking on your feet, or a partner who's perusing information from websites along the way, you can toss in an unscheduled stop. These are the gems. Trust us, you'll eventually get to your planned campsite, but the laughs years later will be over the stop you made at a Podunk gas station, where the owners had a pet goat who stole the hearts of everyone in the car with its antics as it jumped among rocks and over picnic tables.

And never underestimate the power of ducks. They're comical. They're cute—and they don't bite. You can find them in the urban ponds of city centers or outposts in the middle of nowhere. You can feed them crumbs of about anything from your hands, and they'll follow the kids like an army.

These are but a couple of options you may encounter along the route of your family camping trip. On the surface, the goal is to find a place and set up a camp, but deep down, the process is to arrive at a consensus that best accommodates the needs of your family, your group.

Once you've set up your camp, there will be moments when kids are overtired and a meltdown is in order. If it's of any consolation, you've done so well in providing new and stimulating activities that their mental and physical systems have become over-amped. Nature demands the use of our five senses—sometimes all at once—and a little time in the elements can be a lot to process for kids, especially if they're not accustomed to the sudden switch from virtual life and its conveniences to the experiential realms of rain, wind, fish, frogs, and mud.

Be prepared to hold young children and cuddle or have them nap in your arms, or you may have to load them into the car seat and drive loops around the campground while they cry themselves to sleep. It won't take long, and they'll get the sleep that they need.

LET 'EM RUN

On the road to your campsite, where there are safe pullouts or other peripheral attractions along the highway, it pays to stop, even if it seems all is well in the back seat. The idea is to keep the mental momentum on the upswing, and that means switching up the activities well before a crash in attitude. If you're taking a familiar route, you can time your stops in preplanned intervals. With children under 5, an hour can be a long time in the confines of a car seat. Older children won't mind the extra stop, and stretching your legs every hour or so will help keep you alert for the drive ahead. The best places to stop will have a safe parking lot and "soft" hiking trails leading to the woods. These soft trails are defined by a base layer of wood chips, pea gravel, or other soft medium conducive to

Pull over. Open the doors and let them run for a positive mood swing in the camping experience.

running and minimizing injuries from falls. The kids will want to run full out, and it is medicinal.

PACK A SURPRISE

The kids might have thought they'd seen everything that went into the car during the packing cycle, but it sometimes behooves parents to sneak in extra items for when morale takes a turn for the worse. Adding to the downturn is that sometimes one child melting down becomes the catalyst for others to follow and form a back-seat chorus you'd rather not hear again anytime soon.

One solution might be a round of their favorite candy, but be mindful of their metabolism: An extra shot of sugar can sometimes make the situation worse. Some groups make a pact to leave cell phones, tablets, notebooks, and other electronic devices in the car's glove compartment to heighten the sensory experiences and deepen relationships among siblings. If your group has made that pact and you encounter a meltdown, it might not hurt to break down and cheat the system for an hour or two. The same goes for the onboard entertainment screens in the back seat.

New music might trigger a change of heart, or launch a fresh kids' audiobook through the speakers.

Other tacks to try in the moment of meltdown could include surprising them with the gadget bags mentioned elsewhere in this book. For prolonged suspense—and to keep a carrot dangling longer—introduce one item from the gadget bag each day: a magnifying glass on Monday, tweezers on Tuesday, a bright new bandana the next day. Maybe toss in a few bright

Breaking out the goods to blow bubbles can change the attitude of kids who aren't quite digging your plans for the camping experience.

new bundles of paracord they can braid into survival bracelets. If they've already got gadget bags and quite a few of the goods contained therein, try to think of new items to hand out each trip.

Sometimes breaking into a song will do it, especially if you tell them they must continue crying and you don't want to hear anybody laugh. This trick works even better if you can think of a tune that carries context within the family. Maybe it's saying and acting out a lame line from a corny movie. Mimicking their cries back to them has never worked for me, but that isn't to say you shouldn't try it.

ENDURE!

To steal a line from an instructor who was speaking about maintaining mental focus during an emergency in one of my wilderness EMT classes, "It's their pain, not yours." Though the saying comes off harsh on its surface, I've found that in holds merit through the years, especially when it comes to helping me focus on kids' safety. Many times the fracas breaks out when I'm driving, and the one thing that has to go flawless, despite all the turmoil elsewhere in the vehicle, is that I get my wife and kids safely to point B.

It also helps the parent to classify the meltdown, as they come in colors—many colors.

Child against the World: These are usually relegated to just one child, and if you're lucky, one child at a time. It can be almost anything: a wet shoe, no more candy or potato chips, boredom—a stuffed toy fell to the floorboards out of reach from the car seat. In many cases, siblings become your strongest allies, depending upon gender, age and other dynamics in your social camping mix. Strangely enough, these meltdowns commonly resolve themselves. The toy is returned from the floor. You

Sometimes kids melt down and convince you that the end of the world is near. Take a deep breath; it's their pain, not yours. Concentrate. Drive and get them down the road safely.

CHARLIE GOES CAMPING

Years ago a friend and his family had been camping in the Dakotas. They traveled in an over-size station wagon, slept out in a tent at night, and by day they took in the Black Hills, Mount Rushmore, the Badlands, and other points of interest. But the attraction that grabbed the family most began appearing on highway billboards 50 miles out from a small gas station: "Baby Rattlers Ahead." As the family pressed on, the snake-touting billboards continued in a countdown of the miles to the "life-changing" exhibit, which turned out to be a small gas station. After the gas tank had been filled, the family inquired about the baby snakes and was told they were in a pen "out back" of the station. My friend says they approached the display, which resembled a large sandbox, only to find wooden carved and painted oversized rattles, the simple toy given to babies back in the 1950s and 1960s.

It's all in the marketing, and it's all in good fun. Quirky attractions still exist, according to online research. Arizona has "The Thing," a mysterious mummified mother and daughter display; Brandon, Iowa, claims to have one of the country's largest frying pans. The pan measures 14 feet across its bottom, and local lore holds that it can fry 528 eggs or sizzle up 88 pounds of bacon. Cawker City, Kansas, is home of the world's largest ball of sisal twine, and the list of weird attractions goes on and on.

As you develop your family camping repertoire, you may find a perennial favorite place in which to pitch a tent each year, and on the way to that special place you may encounter roadside attractions far less ostentatious than those mentioned above, but places that become a nostalgic part of camping trips as the years roll on.

For me it was the ritual that came with each visit to the Cut Foot Sioux Inn, north of Deer River, Minnesota. Though we left home well prepared with food and other supplies to camp in the national forest campground for several days at a time, we'd always stop at the inn—a

suddenly spot a deer, or a raccoon, and the mood swings back into the positive zone.

Child or Children against Multiple Siblings: We might be told in corporate meetings that conflict is the gateway to opportunity, or you may have heard it rephrased that it's an opportunity for growth. No matter which way the concepts are rendered in the boardroom, opportunity will be the last thing that comes to mind as the backseat bickering or picnic table tantrum escalates between two or more of your beloved campers. Remember that stuffed toy that hodgepodge of rental cabins, a small grocery store, and a gift shop. Dad needed to buy live minnows for fishing, and as he paid for his bait, we kids could toss in our selections of candy.

The key attraction for me those years was that the display case contained the somewhat-hard-to-find Zero candy bars, with their white chocolate outer shell. Far above the glass candy case, a miniature figurine-like clown with a balance pole rode a unicycle on thin copper wire that stretched in a continuous loop along the breadth of the back wall. The Larson family—Kermit, Gladys, and Winton—owned and ran the inn. Each trip north they bedazzled my siblings and me with the battery-powered unicycle display.

More than fifty years later, I still return to that inn as part of my annual visits back to Minnesota. The unicycle display was removed decades ago, and the contents of the candy counter have been abbreviated to just a few selections, none of which come close to the coveted Zero bars.

But it's still worth stopping.

The place began as a carrot dangled before us kids on our trips north. The absence of meltdowns during the 160-mile drive from home to the campground meant access to the ever-decadent candy bars and the chance to marvel at a motorized toy that never fell from a high wire.

Now I purchase shot glasses, coffee mugs, and other memorabilia advertising the little inn, and my mind races back to the days of limber legs, shoulders freckled from the summer sun, and endless hours exploring beaches, fishing the lakes, and discovering secret trails through the towering pines. I try to remember the last time I laughed myself to sleep at night, and all I can come up with is my childhood summers when my mom, dad, and siblings played silly word games in a giant canvas tent.

fell to the floor? In this rendition a sibling, not gravity, is at fault. What's worse; it's recurrent.

"Mom, he threw my teddy bear on the floor again."

"Johnny?"

"He's putting it by my face, and it stinks like pee. He's so annoying."

"Well, can you just pick it up and give it to him?"

Sound familiar? Sure, there's a teachable moment there, somewhere, but you're merging through three lanes of heavy traffic and coming up with zip. If you're lucky enough to have a child to stick between the two combatants, that might work. Sometimes an older third child can help mediate, but if the argument seems to gain momentum with each passing mile, it might be best to pull over at the next rest stop. A physical break in the monotony often gives kids a chance to reset. Hopefully the stimulus of getting everyone out of the car for a dose of fresh air and the chance to stretch their legs or run around for a few minutes will change things up when you get back in the car. If not, these things too eventually will resolve themselves.

Big-Kid Tactics

Lest we make it sound like meltdowns are reserved only for the likes of 5-year-olds, the kid within all of us sometimes comes out—and in negative ways. As a preemptive approach to mitigating meltdowns, it helps to establish that everyone is on board with the family camping experience in the planning stages; and by on board, we don't mean for teenagers to swallow the camping experience in

Kids of all ages love to throw rocks. It's great exercise and a great way to vent.

subservience to authority but to feel ownership in the entire process of what the trip could look like in terms of logistics, fun, and activities.

Giving ownership at the front end of the experience most often translates to accountability later in the trip. For example, a 13-year-old son wants to go to a renowned mountain biking area and the 11-year-old daughter wants to take in a water park. The two activities are an 8-hour drive apart. All parties should be aware of some long-distance driving between the two venues. All parties also should agree to making that drive—and planning for the stops along the way.

Some families establish lead roles among teenage siblings in planning their itineraries weeks ahead of the trip. The premise is that the youths take turns as the family guide for a day. One of them leads the camping experience, including meals, logistics, and activities, for an entire day, and someone else takes a turn the next day. Handing the reins of leadership over to youths during the planning process instills a sense of responsibility that might well fit into homeschooling or other school curricula as real-world applications using history, geography, natural sciences, and math skills, particularly where traveling is involved. You may want to propose that family members work together on a budget that includes calculations for gas, meals, camping fees, and incidental expenses. Activities require time, which presents another logistical calculation. As an added dimension, each of the family guides may want to study up on local geology and historical or interpretive exhibits respective to their sections of the trip.

The memories you make while camping stay with you long after you've returned home.

BACK AT HOME

If you've fallen in love with camping and can't wait to get back out in the hills, it helps to think of home as your support station. With modern amenities such as dishwashers, clothes washers, and dryers, the camping family can regroup and plan for their next camping sojourn in a matter of days. High-speed internet on your home computer makes research a snap when it comes to mapping out routes, setting up itineraries, and working through other logistical details before your

Now that you're home, it's time to dry out and repack your camping gear.

CHAPTER 17

CLEAN UP

YOU'VE GONE CAMPING: You conquered hills, caught fish, picked berries, swam in the lakes, took in local attractions, played games, sang songs together, and marveled in all of nature.

But now you're home. The lawn needs mowing, and a nagging list of other chores awaits. Truth is, however, you're still camping. Perhaps the tent was put away with dew on its tarp. The sleeping bags were damp when you broke camp. The dishes are dirty from a rapid-fire breakfast before you hit the road. All of these conditions spell mold and mildew in the days ahead.

While it would seem that camping chores complicate the issue as the family immerses itself back into everyday life, revitalizing equipment for the next camping trip prolongs the fun of the camping experience you just had and helps focus on the trip ahead.

Depending on the capabilities of your camping family, you might not have to do it all when it comes to the chores of reentry. Delegating tasks such as lugging laundry in from the car, sorting it, and throwing a load in the washer, emptying coolers, and running a load of dishes and utensils in the dishwasher will ease the stress of catching up and allow the family to get into the groove of planning its next trip just that much quicker. Depending on your camping style, you may have an appreciable amount of recyclables that need sorting.

Hint: Never underestimate the power, capability, and motivation of 9-year-olds. Those of you who have them most probably know about their willingness to follow instructions and their ever-present quest to master new challenges.

Another trick to try if your group has made an agreement to camp without phones, tablets, notebooks, or other electronic devices is to do all your texting when you're about an hour away from home. Having caught up on chats, e-mails, and texts, sending pictures via social media before you reach home goes a long way toward hitting the ground running after you've pulled into the driveway.

For some families, the task of putting away the camp will alleviate the melancholy that sometimes sets in with reentry to home life after an ethereal experience in the woods.

TENTS, TARPS, BAGS, AND PADS

A clothesline or the handrail of a porch or stairs makes for a great drying rack upon which to hang the tent, sleeping bags, and pads. A slight breeze works wonders in drying the fabric of camping gear and gives it a fresh smell.

Hanging sleeping bags out to dry after a trip keeps them fresh and free of mold.

A garage works great too, especially when returning home in rainy weather. Inexpensive hooks and eyebolts screwed into the ceiling make handy places to hang tents, tarps, and other equipment.

CLOTHING AND SHOES

If you've tossed dirty laundry into a plastic trash bag for the past several days of your camping trip, be prepared for the aroma of adventures past. The rich smell of woodsmoke lingering on the camp laundry may rekindle the great memories you made on your outing. A ketchup stain on a shirt, for example, may bring back laughs over some incident while eating around the campfire. Some folks use a designated set of shirts, pants, and outer wear for their camping adventures. Socks often speak more loudly of camping fun than other clothing, as denoted by copious amounts of mud or sand after a trip. You may want to wash and dry camping clothes separately, which adds to the efficiency when it comes time to pack for the next trip.

Some camping situations require a preamble to tossing clothing into a washing machine. Running an outdoor hose over sandy or muddy zippers, pants, and socks removes a lot of the heavy soil and adds life to your washer and dryer.

Most campers pack a variety of footwear, and hiking boots will need drying out, as will sandals and other shoes. Crumpled-up newspaper stuffed inside hiking boots draws out moisture from their inner reaches, and some campers like to freshen their boots up by adding a scented anticling dryer sheet. Sandals also require attention to ensure that their webbing or leather dries completely, sooner than later. An inspection of your footgear in the drying process can alert you to worn laces, ripped stitching in the uppers, or cracks or other compromises to the soles.

Machine-washing other types of sneakers or shoes with synthetic uppers is a judgment call. Some models may have glues or other compounds holding in padded inserts, and a washing machine—though it gets shoes very clean—may deconstruct the innards and compromise the fit.

COOKWARE AND FOOD

Depending on how you put up the dishes when you broke camp, these might also benefit from a bout under the garden hose before placing them in the dishwasher. Isolating camp dishes and running them in the dishwasher as a separate load offers vast benefits when it comes to not forgetting items when you pack for the next outing. After they've dried, wrap coffee cups, glass bowls, and other breakable vessels in several layers of newspaper; then arrange them in your plastic tote or other container. The newspaper protects coffee mugs from breakage, and the newspaper makes great fire starter for your next camp. As you unpack the camp cooking utensils and prepare them for washing, start a list of items you missed on your last trip. Maybe it's time to replace that aged hand-crank can opener—or maybe you forgot to pack a can opener in the first place. The list goes on and on at our house as we make continual improvements to what we need for a better dining experience out at camp.

Spices

Spices sometimes fall victim to rainy weather or high humidity. The steak seasoning that sprinkled so smoothly from the container on day two of your trip may have become a dense clod that rattles around in its container by the time you get home. You can often shake and break up the clods, and if you can access the spices by removing the lid, try tossing in two dozen grains of dry white rice. As for table salt, it's often easier to toss it out, refill the container, and add the grains of rice. The dry rice won't compromise flavor, and it works as a moisture magnet to help keep spices dry during times of high humidity where you live and keeps the good stuff flowing should the weather turn inclement during your next trip. Some spices come in metal cans. Given the acidity of some spices and the corrosive characteristic of most salts, the inside of these cans can rust over time. It's best to relegate these spices to plastic containers, ideally transparent ones that make it easy to identify them in low-light cooking conditions out at camp. You may want to buy a set of small plastic containers that hold just enough spices for an outing and label them as a set. Camping and outdoor supply stores often sell kits that can be loaded with your favorite flavorings.

CHECK FOR CRITTERS

Now that you're home, it's time to inspect your body like never before. Though you may have used DEET and other repellents as your daily protection against critters that can cause health problems that ruin your camping trip and beyond, bath time upon returning home should take on new significance, particularly if your bathroom has bright lighting and mirrors. Most states, especially in the Midwest and the East, have populations of deer ticks, which are prime agents in spreading the bacteria that causes Lyme disease. These ticks are terribly small for the damage they inflict, and a couple of my outdoor-loving cousins have had to endure Lyme disease despite their daily inspections for ticks. Depending on your family dynamic and comfort zones among siblings, a crosscheck among siblings, spouses, etc., can add an extra level of protection. Look and feel carefully behind the ears, where hair thins near the neck, in the depths of the armpits, the backs

Where there are deer there are deer ticks (also known as black-legged ticks). Check yourself and pets carefully for these tiny ticks, which carry bacteria that cause Lyme disease.

of knees, and other crannies. As kids, our parents parted through our hair every night before we headed to bed, and at home it was up to us to check ourselves out. I found dog ticks or wood ticks numerous times before they could do any damage, except for once; I'll leave it to your imagination where that enlarged tick had made an unsavory camp and engorged on my blood.

In many states, mosquitoes, blackflies, chiggers, gnats, and flying bugs smaller than a pinhead cause major welts. These welts usually surround a tiny wound where the bug bit, and they need to weep out before the swelling subsides. A hot shower or bath makes a perfect time to rub scabs off softened skin and squeeze out fluids that could cause infection if the wound were allowed to seal up. The best time to ease the swelling and draw out toxins is when the wound is open. Apply a small amount of antibiotic ointment and a Band-Aid. The absorbent part of the bandage and the ointment will keep the bite from sealing back up and will draw out fluids that can turn septic.

Pets

Besides the obvious search for ticks and other parasites, particularly around the ears, be aware that pets often attract plant pests on even a brief outdoor adventure. Mainly it's the seeds of some plants that can plague your dog or cat and leave your pet looking like its chosen dreadlocks for its new style. It's no fun for your beloved pets, and it's a chore for you to get the burs out of their coat, but it's a must. I used to have it in for the plants that seemed hell-bent on ruining the coats of our pets until I took some college courses in natural sciences and learned about "advanced plant strategies." The ensuing study examined the mechanisms by which plants ensure their propagation through an evolution of seed structure so that their seeds stick to animals and eventually fall off and take root in fertile ground. Having an attitude that "plants are people too" may ease the snipping, clipping, and brushing you end up doing to bring

Check dogs for ticks, and sticky plant seeds, when you get home.

your pet back to normal after a brush with the burs. Most camping locales have leash laws, which help keep pets in proximity to the owners, but some do not. Knowing local plant life before letting Fido out for a quick run can save you from major grooming problems.

NEWFOUND FRIENDS

Yet another way to prolong the camping experience when you're back home is to organize the names and numbers of people you met on your trip and put them into proper context. These are the folks who showed up around your campfire on a whim, only to discover they are best friends with your cousin who lives in another state, the flurry of people who came from their campsites to help you retrieve your keys when you locked them in your car, the couple who found and returned your puppy when it got lost in the woods. The relationships built from these impromptu in-camp experiences are heartfelt, and they're real.

But you meet a lot of people these days, and chances are these newfound camping friends are only known by an uncommon area code and phone number in the text log of your phone. Or maybe you scribbled their names and numbers on a business card or across the flap of a cereal box. Take time now to put them into your contacts or add them as friends or followers on your social media accounts. Chances are you'll run into them again—camping has way of reuniting folks with a love for families and friends in the great outdoors.

CHARLIE GOES CAMPING

"Everybody take an armful." That's the voice of my mom when we pulled into the driveway of our urban home after a family camping trip. Every camping trip. There would be three bushels of laundry, a large cardboard box of dishes and utensils, a cooler with soggy leftover groceries, damp sleeping bags, and maybe a wet tent—all of which had to be dealt with before our next outing. We'd emerge from the car after the long drive home from the campground, arms laden with clothing, food, and keepsakes, mainly interesting rocks, that we'd gathered from the lakeshore.

Though she used the singular version of the word "armful," there would be many armfuls of stuff to be carted into the garage, the house, and the backyard before we staged our supplies for the next trip.

On top of that, Mom and Dad formed a family business: Driftwood Ornamentals. The day before we returned home on each camping trip, we'd scour the beaches of a large lake and collect ornate pieces of driftwood. Mom and Dad would order hundreds of dozens of plastic flowers and make arrangements that they'd sell during winter. I don't know that we ever needed the extra money, but it was just one more activity to cement us tighter together as a family. Back to the chores, my bother Chris and I would unload armload after armload of driftwood from the bottom of the boat we towed behind the family car and stack it carefully so that it would dry in time for winter.

Dad would return to his shifts as an air traffic controller, and Mom and we kids would prepare for our next outing. She loved the outdoor life and recognized the connective tissue that camping instilled in us siblings and our parents, but what we kids saw mostly was a strong sense of pride as she lined the cardboard box with fresh newspaper and carefully arranged the dishes and utensils for the future. We had a clothesline in the yard, and we'd hang the sleeping bags out in the hot afternoon sun to freshen them up before rolling and packing them back into their respective stuff sacks.

Most amazing to us kids, however, was the rock tumbler. When the immediate unpacking chores were completed and Dad came home from work, we siblings would sort our favorite rocks in small piles then load the tumbler, which was a steel drum that spun incessantly 24 hours a day with a wet grit that polished our rocks smooth as glass. Though we were primarily looking for agates, which polish up to reveal translucent colors and rings of contrasting colors, an untold number of other interesting rocks caught our eyes. We hauled them home, tumbled them smooth, and adorned our shelves and windowsills with our treasures.

Journaling offers an extra dimension to the camping experience. Take in the scene. Write or draw for the added element of what it all means. Introspect.

CHAPTER 18

JOURNAL AND REFLECT

IT'S HARD TO BEAT a pack of unlined index cards, an empty journal or notebook, a few stubby pencils, and a waterproof bag to contain them as part of essential camping gear. The cards may come in handy for making a list of supplies that you want to include on your next camping trip, or for leaving a note back at camp to inform the rest of your camping party that you are attempting a solo hike over the top of Sasquatch Pass.

But the cards often become so much more, especially as conduits to reflecting on the outdoor experience—and in some instances the cards become the foundation of a novel-length piece of literature or other work inspired by experiences in the outdoors. The beauty of index cards is that they offer the unique quality of interchangeability in their sequencing. An afterthought is never an afterthought when you can jot it down on a card and insert it into the appropriate gap between other cards in the sequence.

The cards are also handy for drawing comic sequences, sketches, storyboards, or other sequential creations. Bind them together with small steel paper clamps or oversize paper clips, or punch holes at their tops and bind them with brass fasteners.

Or hand them out to family members in a competition to see who can fold one into the best paper airplane.

To facilitate outdoor reflection with large groups, I like to hand the cards out in twos and threes to each student; instruct them to find a secluded spot in the woods to write, draw, rap, or rhyme; and meet me back at the campfire in an hour. What comes back is never short of amazing in terms of prose, poems, songs, sketches, and other forms of creative expression.

OTHER JOURNALING SUPPLIES

Other writing aids include empty notebooks, sketchbooks, or hardbound journals with thick unlined paper. Many of these are constructed with sturdy bindings and a cover that binds them shut. There are plenty of waterproof pocket journals out there as well.

Nature has a way of bringing out the best in us. But the memories of our experiences become fleeting as the camping trip fades into the days behind us and we reenter the busyness of school, work, and other obligations far from the woods. The extra dimension in personal growth that outdoor experiences impart within us might be lost without some tangible way of recording our thoughts.

That's why we journal.

Or scrapbook. Hobby and craft shops offer no shortage of hardbound, heavy-papered scrapbooks in a seemingly infinite assortment of colors, shapes, and sizes. They also sell glue, feathers, grass, twines, beads, rubber stamping supplies, small tiles, and other decorations to accompany your pictures, tiny seashells, snails, leaves, and other camping memorabilia between the thick pages of the book. If you run short of choices at your local craft shop, go online to find thousands of ideas and sources of supplies. Who knows, scrapbooking may become an extension of your family camping experience in the dark winter months at home. Gather around the table with your scrapbooking supplies, enjoy popcorn, reminisce about the year behind, and plan your camping trips for the year ahead.

Sometimes the camping experience causes us to return home to build mini shrines within the house or out in the yard. These may be an arrangement of rocks, seashells, sticks, stones, driftwood, fur, feathers, fishing lures, and other keepsakes we've lugged from the woods. They take us back to the essence of our camping experience and become the talismans of memories we fear we might lose.

Seashells collected at the beach during a coastal camping trip often adorn windowsills, the headboards of beds, and other places in the home that commemorate the magical places we've camped.

Reflection in the form of journaling often falls to the whims of individuals within the group or family. Some process their camping experiences by writing or drawing; others integrate them in a way that doesn't manifest itself in visible expression. In some families the opposite may be true, and members may want to try putting a collective entry of words or pictures to paper.

Revisiting the fundamentals of storytelling can reveal distinct ways of recounting our experiences to ourselves. What happens to the character—and what it means to the character. And that character, by the way, is you.

Some journal writers expound upon the specifics of wind directions, highway numbers and a map of roads traveled, the number and species of fish caught, and other experiences tallied up around the camp—these entries mean more to their writers, and interpretation remains locked within the mind of the beholder. Other journal writers enter information that delves into the deep-down feelings of how outdoor experiences have moved them. A fire represents warmth, inspiration. A waterfall may mark the irreversible passage of time. Some journal entries may include a combination of both and, taken to the extreme, become publishable, classic outdoor essays.

What was the high point of your last trip? Your last night together as a family on the beach? It's never too early to plan for the next trip—and the good times ahead.

CHAPTER 19

PLAN FOR THE NEXT ONE

YOU'VE ARRIVED at the final chapter. That means a lot to us who put this book together and know well the inspirational, motivational, and medicinal attributes of camping. What's next? If you've followed us through the previous chapters, chances are you've learned a lot about picking your campsite, choosing your shelter, figuring out layers of clothing, securing safe sources of water, keeping yourselves in good company, and nourishing your bodies with the right kind of food. Though we'll give you a few more suggestions, this is the chapter *you* write, where you grow, where you evolve. Family camping is all about the elements of the outdoors and how they intertwine with you, your personalities, your strengths—individually and with one another—and drive you forward into the future.

To some, time becomes a monster, a clock ticking toward mortality at its end. But if you've followed us this far, you've discovered the antithesis: the life-giving, celebratory slowing of time in the woods or mountains, on the lakes or rivers—around campfires where you've watched the glow of fire in the eyes of your children or other loved ones.

There are dozens of axioms about fleeting time and savoring it with others on vacation or in other settings, but nothing can be sweeter than sitting down and planning the next trip into the outdoors.

In one word: Imagine.

Going forward, it helps to consider the essence of the outing you just experienced. What was the most magical moment, the moment when you most felt connected with the outdoors and the others around you, satisfied, fulfilled? Take some time thinking about this one. The logistics and specifics of the next trip should be predicated upon reflections of your recent camping experience.

The journaling we described in chapter 18 often comes in handy as a reference to accessing the deep-down, elemental ingredients we glean from camping, and the exploration of thoughts can often define the ingredients we hope to reap from future outings. Was it the food, the activities, the setting and friends—the time away from a daily grind? Was it the feeling of mastery when we lashed together a makeshift shelter with poles, a tarp, and paracord? Or was it that our camp setting provided an environment where we as family members were captive to one another?

These questions are the grist for growth. Putting your finger on the answers can help in planning the next trip. For example, you planned to focus on hiking and biking activities in your last outing, but on a whim you took a side trip to a water park and agree as a family that the exhilaration of a large slide was the high point of the trip. Maybe the activities for your next camping trip should include an excursion to another water park, or you might all wind up ziplining across a canyon.

SETTING AS CHARACTER

An old fiction writer's trick holds that in every good novel or movie, nature constitutes an extra character. Many writers are campers and know how we, as characters, are tied inextricably to the land—and that the land moves us. This is the stuff that drives the poetry and prose of classic outdoor essays, books, and movies. Western novels and movies capitalize on this concept by having heroes riding through sandstone canyons with the bad guys silhouetted on a high ridge. The wind-honed rock outcroppings complement the plight of the main character, who may be alone, searching. On a mission.

Hiking and camping along a densely wooded sector of the Appalachian Trail might provide the perfect setting for rediscovering companionship with an old high school chum. Or, as a family, you might want to explore the vast open stretches of the West. Whatever those impulses, let the land and elements guide you.

These two sisters wanted a beach for the backdrop of their trip. Planning to camp in an ecosystem that has special meaning heightens the experience.

MAKE LISTS

To delve deeper into the mechanical aspects of your next trip, list making may prove essential to remembering the things you need—and leaving behind the stuff you never use. Though you can scribble or print them out like household grocery shopping lists, it helps to think of camping lists as a living, evolving tool that you can modify as your camping experience morphs and, along with it, your needs for different equipment at different locations, different activities, and other details.

Some campers prefer jotting down forgotten items or "wish lists" on napkins or empty food containers as revelations come to them during the trip, then adding those items to computer spreadsheets at home. Yet others prefer weathered notebooks or cardboard or write out their list of future supplies and details on campground receipts or across non-pertinent sections of maps. To some, planning of any kind tarnishes the entire camping experience.

Yet others bring their spreadsheets with them as apps on their phones, tablets, or other electronic devices and modify them on the spot. To those who like to organize and plan, lists can not only include itemized equipment and groceries but also columns containing contact numbers for campground or tour operators and rental agencies for boats and other outdoor gear. Campers who prefer using phones, tablets, or other electronic devices can insert live links to websites for reserving their campsites; accessing maps, permits, and other information; and just about anything else they'll need to know on the go.

As for organizing the lists in a spreadsheet, try designating a column near the left for the information associated with picking a location and reserving campsite, then add tabs to accommodate basic camping equipment with entries such as tents, cots, pads, bags, pillows, tarps, and other associated equipment. Another column can be dedicated to food and water and include cooking pots, pans, dishes, utensils, and the hardware associated with eating and dedicating the column immediately to the right of it for ingredients, condiments, prepared foods, beverages, and snacks. Camping lists generally delineate themselves between the supplies associated with the immediate sleeping and eating experience and items or details needed for peripheral activities.

If fishing dominates the daily activities, a new tab in the sheet can be dedicated to rods, reels, leaders, line, baits, and other relevant equipment. Rock climbing has its own exhaustive list of supplies and equipment, as do hunting, bicycling, and canoeing, kayaking, and other water sports.

Backpacking may deserve a tab of its own, as all the equipment, food, and other supplies must fit neatly onto your back for multiple days. Items to include in this subcategory are ultralight tents, bags and pads, small titanium cockpits, and lightweight utensils, miniature camp stoves, small containers of fuel, freeze-dried foods, items that weigh mere ounces and can be nested within one another—and the infamous sawed-off toothbrush.

Logistics for the different trips deserve a column. Set up a column or tab for quick access to phone numbers for federal campground reservations and backcountry permits; phone numbers for private campgrounds; and phone numbers and other contact information for zipline operators, sightseeing tours, recorded information and updates on weather and highway conditions, canoe and kayak rentals, and water park operators. Toss in your emergency contact numbers for relatives and doctors while you're at it. Also include contact numbers of the parents of your kids' friends and make note of any allergies, medications (and their schedules), and outlying medical conditions.

Medications, prescriptions, and first-aid items deserve a column of their own. EpiPens and other epinephrine injectors can't be frozen and have expiration dates worth noting in your database.

If spreadsheets aren't for you, use the following list as a template. Place the book facedown on a copier and copy the pages. Add or subtract items as they apply to your particular trip or your needs.

Sleep
Location:
☐ Permits (for backpacking areas)
☐ Campground reservation/registration
☐ Weather forecast

Shelter

- ☐ Tent
- ☐ Tent poles
- ☐ Rainfly
- ☐ Paracord
- ☐ Stakes
- ☐ Hatchet or hammer
- ☐ Camping saw
- ☐ Ground cloth for inside the tent
- ☐ Cot
- ☐ Sleeping pad
- ☐ Sleeping bag
- ☐ Pillow
- ☐ Hammock

Clothing

- ☐ Under layers
- ☐ Socks
- ☐ Middle layers
- ☐ Outer layers
- ☐ Windbreaker
- ☐ Rain jacket
- ☐ Rain pants
- ☐ Boots
- ☐ Shoes
- ☐ Sandals
- ☐ Hats
- ☐ Caps
- ☐ Sunscreen
- ☐ Sunglasses
- ☐ Scarves/neck rings
- ☐ Gloves/mittens
- ☐ Bath towels
- ☐ Swim suits
- ☐ Duffel bags
- ☐ Backpacks

Eat/Drink

☐ Water filter
☐ Purification tablets or drops
☐ Water containers
☐ Bladder packs
☐ Pots
☐ Pans
☐ Dutch oven
☐ Dishes
☐ Cups
☐ Utensils (forks, spoons, sporks, and knives)
☐ Spatulas
☐ Tongs
☐ Washbasins
☐ Dish soap
☐ Washcloth
☐ Towels or paper towels
☐ Coolers
☐ Trash bags
☐ Toilet paper
☐ Electrolyte mix
☐ Entrees
☐ Snacks
☐ Finger food
☐ Spices
☐ Butter
☐ Cooking oils
☐ Aluminum foil
☐ Hot pads/oven mitts

Play

☐ Gadget bags
☐ Magnifying glass
☐ Mineral lens (very small and available at hobby shops)
☐ Binoculars
☐ Compass
☐ Maps

- [ ] Lines of different diameters and lengths
- [ ] Climbing web
- [ ] Carabiners (4)
- [ ] Index cards
- [ ] Journal
- [ ] Pencils
- [ ] Pencil sharpener (small, not battery powered)

Camp Life Hacks
- [ ] Lines
- [ ] Duct tape
- [ ] First-aid kit/survival kit
- [ ] Shower kit
- [ ] Personal flotation devices
- [ ] Wild plant identification book
- [ ] Pet leashes
- [ ] Survival knife

ABOUT THE AUTHOR AND PHOTOGRAPHER

Charlie Ess grew up camping in Minnesota and left the north woods for the far north woods, mountains, and oceans of Alaska in 1978. Charlie met his wife, Cheryl, in 1980 when she hired him to help with her commercial fishing operation out at False Pass on Unimak Island, which is the first in the 1,200-mile string of the Aleutian Islands. Charlie has been writing for magazines, newspapers, and other publications every month since 1993 and has been the North Pacific bureau chief for *National Fisherman* since 1998. In addition to his writing life, Charlie has

facilitated experiential outdoor activities for the past fifteen years with students at the Alaska Job Corps Center and through the Anchorage-based Rural Alaska Community Action Program, where he coordinates an AmeriCorps program.

Photographer **Cheryl Ess** came to Alaska decades before Charlie, as a 4-year-old along with her mom, dad, and three siblings in 1959 as part of a group of adventurous Midwesterners who came north to prove up on homesteads and carve out a life in the nation's last frontier. Cheryl's career in photography stems back to the early 1970s when she began shooting Kodachrome through an Olympus OM-1. She frequently publishes photos in *National Fisherman* magazine, *Alaska* magazine, and numerous other publications. Samples of her work can be viewed at SnowshoeMedia.com.

Charlie and Cheryl live in Sutton, Alaska. For more information, visit Snowshoe Media.com.